THE
Imperative Is Leadership

THE

Imperative Is

LEADERSHIP

A Report on Ministerial Development
in the Christian Church (Disciples of Christ)

By Carroll C. Cotten

Director, Study on Ministerial Education
in the Christian Church (Disciples of Christ)

With Recommendations by the
STUDY COMMISSION ON MINISTERIAL EDUCATION
Christian Church (Disciples of Christ)
Frank G. Dickey, Chairman

THE BETHANY PRESS • ST. LOUIS, MISSOURI

Library of Congress Cataloging in Publication Data

Disciples of Christ. Study Commission on Ministerial
Education.
    The imperative is leadership.

    Includes bibliographical references.
    1. Theology—Study and teaching—Disciples of
Christ. 2. Disciples of Christ—Clergy. I. Cotten,
Carroll C., 1936-   II. Title.
BX7311.D57   230'. 6'6   73-8893
ISBN 0-8272-1604-1

Distributed by The G. R. Welch Company, Toronto, Ontario, Canada.

Imperative for Leadership

One of the keys to the future of the church is a leadership that is dedicated, dynamic, creative, and innovative. It is a leadership that is attuned to both the will and purpose of God and the needs and challenges of the world. The church must give priority to highly qualified leaders—laity and clergy—who are committed to the church and its mission. The fulfillment of the church's mission depends upon its leadership.

This imperative catches up the concerns for the laity, the ministry and higher education. The concept of the laity must be elevated from membership to ministry, as God's servant-people in the world. At the same time the order of the ministry, the professional minister, must be enhanced and provision made for a vigorous program of recruitment, guidance, and continuous education. The need for openness towards prophetic and creative leaders is recognized. The church's ministry is a continuation and extension of Christ, her Lord. God raises up his ministers for such a time as this.

"Report of the Committee for 1970 and Beyond to the Christian Church (Disciples of Christ)." Adopted by the General Assembly, Seattle, Washington, 1969.

Contents

CONTENTS

Tables and charts

CHARTS:

Foreword

The relationship of a profession to the society it serves is an ever-changing one, for, as the society develops, it is inevitable that the profession must take account of that development if it is to continue to be effective. This fact has been recognized in most professions, with the result that comprehensive appraisals, surveys, or studies have been made from time to time to determine how effectively a given profession is meeting its current and prospective responsibilities. The most productive of these studies have also given attention to the educational programs leading to professional status and have made suggestions and recommendations for strengthening these educational programs.

It was in the light of these considerations that the General Board of the Christian Church (Disciples of Christ), in 1969, authorized the study that is reported in this volume. In order to carry out the objectives in the minds of the members of the General Board, a Study Commission was appointed with the authorization to employ a staff and proceed with the study.

The study speaks for itself; however, it seems appropriate with the completion of the study to express appreciation to the commission members, to the staff, and to all of those who have assisted in the preparation of this report. Special thanks should be given to Carroll Cotten, who served as director for the study. He has worked diligently and effectively to bring this study to its conclusion, and hearty thanks are owed to him.

The full value of a study of this kind often becomes more apparent as the years go by. It is our hope that such will be the case with this report. While its comprehensive treatment of the main aspects of education for the professional ministry in the Christian Church has a value that one can see immediately, the effect of many of the recommendations that the commission is making may not be visible for some years. The commission hopes, of course, that its recommendations will appear so sound as to be readily acceptable, and that, once accepted, their effects will be such as to cause future generations of the profession to speak of them with appreciation.

It is the desire of the Study Commission that this study be dedicated to Dr. Harlie Smith, former president of the Board of Higher Education, Christian Church (Disciples of Christ), who for many years dreamed of such a study and whose wisdom and leadership lighted the way for this report.

On behalf of the members of the Study Commission, I welcome the opportunity to express our appreciation to all who have contributed to this important study.

FRANK G. DICKEY
Chairman, Study Commission on
Ministerial Education

Acknowledgments

This study of ministerial education has directly involved over two hundred persons. It is impossible to express personal appreciation for the important contribution each has made. However, I wish to express my gratitude to some who have made significant contributions to this study:

To William Miller, president of the Board of Higher Education, who through creative administration provided the resources and released the personal energy making this study possible.

To Frank Dickey, chairman of the Study Commission, who guided the unfolding process of our thinking into careful written articulation with admirable skill and constant graciousness.

To Donald Browning, vice-chairman of the Study Commission, for leadership of critical work sessions in subcommittee combined with an inspiring grasp and articulation of our total effort.

To all members of the Study Commission, who worked diligently and insightfully for the Christian Church with little personal gain.

To our consultants, who provided expertise and insight which gave wisdom and balance to our efforts.

To the administrators, faculty, and students of related colleges, universities, and theological schools for their kind hospitality and cooperation during campus visits and the sharing of honest facts and feelings.

To those who provided financial and moral support, without whom this study would not have been possible.

To Dode Bryan, research assistant, whose personal dedication to this study and unstinting cooperation were essential to its completion and a source of inspiration to all of us.

ACKNOWLEDGMENTS

To the entire staff of the Board of Higher Education, in particular to Barton Updike, for koinonia and agape expressed through the sharing of professional insights and personal friendships which influenced and supported both the study and its director.

CARROLL COTTEN

March 1, 1973
Fresno, California

Introduction

In July, 1969, the General Board of the Christian Church (Disciples of Christ)[1] authorized an objective and comprehensive study on ministerial education. The Administrative Committee of the General Board defined the purpose and scope of the study and assigned the oversight of the study to the church's Board of Higher Education.[2] That division appointed a ten-member Study Commission on Ministerial Education broadly representative of the total church. Consultants were added where needed.[3]

When sufficient funds for the study had been pledged,[4] Randall West, then vice moderator of the church, presented a charge to the commission on behalf of the General Board, and the statement of purpose and scope was examined. Central questions of the study were articulated and a schedule of research and meetings for analysis of the research was established. A "central issues" questionnaire was administered to a selected, representative sample of ten major publics among the Disciples. Returns generally confirmed that the concerns the commission considered central reflected the major concerns of the denomination. A selected list of these issues is given to indicate the direction and scope of the commission's inquiry.[5]

Including the first meeting, the Study Commission met five times as a

1. To avoid unnecessary repetition, the Christian Church (Disciples of Christ) is referred to in various ways throughout the report: Christian Church, the church, the Disciples, and the denomination.

2. See Appendix A for statement of purpose and scope.

3. See Appendix C for roster of commission and consultants.

4. See Appendix B for sources and amounts of pledges.

5. See Appendix D.

total group and four times in subcommittees. In addition, a series of progress reports was made to:

1. The directors of the Board of Higher Education
2. The Council of Ministers (regional ministers and chief executives of general units)
3. The Administrative Committee of the General Board
4. A meeting of presidents and deans of graduate theological institutions related to the church
5. The Commission on Brotherhood Finance (national agency for allocation of the church's contributions to concerns beyond local congregations)

The work of the Study Commission included a variety of research methods:

1. Examination of the major literature on education for ministry that has been written in the last ten years, in addition to earlier, classical works, including eight studies of education for ministry by other denominations.
2. Examination of institutional documents and records, including college and seminary catalogs, self-studies, financial records, student records, and descriptions of educational programs.
3. Personal and group interviews with more than 135 students, faculty, administrators, ministers (congregational, regional, general), lay persons, and researchers.
4. Visits to the campuses of all eight institutions of graduate theological education related to the church, three related undergraduate institutions of higher education, and five seminaries not related to the church.[6]
5. Administration and analysis of two questionnaires with a total of more than two thousand respondents.
6. Analysis of institutional and student data that have been collected over the past ten years by the Board of Higher Education.
7. Analysis of data describing various aspects of the Christian Church. Major sources included the *Year Book* of the Christian Church, financial records from the Commission on Brotherhood Finance and Unified Promotion, in addition to studies conducted by the Department of Ministry and Worship and the Pension Fund.

---

6. Related educational institutions are those holding membership in the Board of Higher Education of the Christian Church.

1

The Christian Church:
Nature, Purpose, and Ministry

Any denominational study of ministerial education should include some examination of the denomination's self-understanding regarding its nature, purpose, and ministry. However, since it is a noncreedal church, it is difficult for the Christian Church to articulate its theology clearly and authoritatively.

It seems that the current self-understanding of the church is articulated primarily through resolutions and policy documents, most of which are approved at biennial assemblies attended by delegates representative of the whole body. Therefore, the theology of the Christian Church is, by its nature, political and in constant process of change, reflecting emerging consensus among the diverse publics that constitute the denomination.

Recent resolutions and documents, particularly the *Provisional Design of the Christian Church (Disciples of Christ),* adopted at the Kansas City General Assembly in 1968, and *Policies and Criteria for the Order of Ministry in the Christian Church (Disciples of Christ),* approved by the Louisville General Assembly in 1971, reveal a consensus regarding the nature, purpose, and ministry of the church. The following summarizes some of these concepts:

Nature of the church. The Christian Church is a voluntary association of persons and social structures that believe in and proclaim Jesus Christ as the primary authority of their personal and collective lives. Thus, the life, ministry, and teachings of Jesus are normative for the church.

Purpose of the church. The purpose of the Christian Church is to participate in and express the ministry of Jesus in a responsible, authentic, and effective manner. That ministry is primarily conceived as servanthood to Christ and the world.

Corporate ministry. Through membership in the church, every Christian is inducted into the corporate ministry of the Christian Church and the Church Universal. By sharing in the corporate ministry, every Christian fulfills his own calling as a servant of Christ. That corporate ministry is characterized by:

1. Public worship of God
2. Care for the common life of the whole body of the church
3. Mediation of God's love to the life of all persons (to individuals and to social structures) through loving service, particularly at points of greatest human need, and primarily through the daily work of the total body of the church

Ordained ministry. In addition, the Christian Church recognizes and authorizes an order of ministry, called of God, set apart or ordained, representative of the church, *to lead and equip the whole church community to fulfill its corporate ministry.*

Restructure. The nature of the Church Universal and its ministry remains constant through history, but its mission of authentic servanthood necessitates adaption of its organizational structures and styles of ministry to the needs and patterns of a changing world.

Modes of ministry. Current leadership functions reflect historic modes of ministry within the Church Universal:

1. Teacher—transmitting the Christian tradition from one generation to another
2. Preacher—interpreting the Scriptures and their continuing relevance to humankind
3. Evangelist—proclaiming the gospel of Christ
4. Priest—administering the sacraments, leading in worship
5. Pastor-Administrator—serving to maintain a company of Christians in continuity with the life and faith of the apostles
6. Prophet—acting as a pioneer and leader in the church's reconciling mission in the world

The above concepts of the purpose of the church and its ministry are commonly shared among most denominations of the Church Universal. There are, however, emphases and structural patterns that have historically characterized the Disciples. It might be useful to discuss a selected number of these emphases that have important implications for ministerial education.

Ecumenism. Beginning with Thomas Campbell, one of the founding fathers of the Disciples, and continuing to the present day, there has existed the conviction that the Church Universal is "essentially, intentionally, and constitutionally one." A passion for the church to express its unity in its structure and function has placed the Christian Church in important roles of leadership in the ecumenical movement. Its contribution to the ecumenical movement has been far greater than might be expected from a church of its size.

Wholeness of ministry. In similar fashion, the Disciples have maintained the conviction that the ministry of the church must retain an adequate expression of its wholeness, fulfilling the enduring modes of ministry (teacher, evangelist, preacher, priest, pastor-administrator, and prophet), which comprise the ministry of Christ.

Ministry of the laity. Disciples have historically emphasized the importance of the ministry of the laity. This has been expressed in several ways: (1) the importance of elders, deacons, and deaconesses in the total life of the congregation; (2) strains of anticlericalism in many sectors of the church, including resistance to a professionally employed clergy; (3) broad involvement of laity in decision-making among all manifestations of the church.

Learned leadership. From Alexander Campbell to the present, the Disciples have always sought a well-educated leadership, both lay and clergy. This emphasis has been the primary force in the creation of many Bible schools, colleges, universities, and seminaries across the years and throughout the United States, Canada, and the world.

Importance of the congregation. The Christian Church has historically maintained the congregation as the basic organizational unit of the church through which its corporate ministry is to be expressed. Since about 1955, the church has been undergoing a process of restructure, producing a provisional design that reaffirms this principle. Three organizational manifestations of the church—congregational, regional, and general—are recognized. Each manifestation is characterized by its integrity, self-governance, authority, rights, and responsibilities. For the general and regional manifestations to function, they must receive financial support from congregations which voluntarily relate themselves to the life of these manifestations of the church. The purposes of the regional and general manifestations are: (1) to extend the corporate ministry of the church in ways impossible for congregations by relating them to the worldwide mission and witness of the total denomination and the Church Universal; (2) to assist and nurture congregations in a variety of ways in order to strengthen their ministry. One evidence of the predominance of the congregation in the structure of the church is that 85% of the operational dollar of the church is used by congregations for their local programs while 15% is used by the regional and general manifestations of the church.

Among the varieties of ministries performed by those who have standing in the order of ministry of the church, those performing congregationally based ministries are numerically predominant. For example, in 1971, 77.4% of all ministers with standing were congregational ministers as distinct from regional, general, institutional, educational, or ecumenical ministers.[1]

These emphases, in various combinations, have influenced considerably the daily life and work of the Christian Church. They tend to produce a church having the following characteristics:

1. *Voluntarism:* membership and participation in the church on the basis of free choice, with a readiness to support that which seems reasonable and a corresponding resistance to any appearance of coercion affecting free choice.

2. *Lay Control:* primary authority of members in directing the life of their own congregation with a corresponding resistance to domination by the professional ministry or imposition of hierarchical authority of any type.

3. *Localism:* the focusing of religious experience, value, and ministry in the life of congregations with a corresponding lack of concern among a majority of lay persons about denominational or ecumenical developments except as these affect congregational life.

4. *Corporate Action with Conviction:* by virtue of the above characteristics, when the Christian Church acts corporately, that action expresses the realization of a common or dominant mind as opposed to deference to ecclesiastical legislation, mechanization, or pressure. Thus, these actions carry the force of corporate conviction and corresponding support.[2]

1. Retired ministers, students, and unclassified ministers not included in this statistic.
2. See "Response to *A Plan of Union for the Church of Christ Uniting* from the Christian Church (Disciples of Christ)," *The Christian* (August 13, 1972), pp. 5, 6.

2

The State of the Christian Church

A. OBJECTIVE DATA

A study of various indicators of the dimensions of the church in the United States and Canada from 1961 to 1971 is given in table 1.

TABLE 1
DIMENSIONS OF THE CHURCH

Category of Analysis	1961	1971	% Comparison
Participating membership	1,379,110	887,845	Decreased 35.6%
Participating congregations	5,186	3,895	Decreased 24.9%
Average participating membership per participating congregation	266	228	Decreased 14.3%
Total additions	101,931	57,603	Decreased 43.5%
Ministers in standing[1]	6,144	5,328	Decreased 13.3%
Pastors of congregations[2]	4,456	3,768	Decreased 15.4%
Other ministers of congregations[3]	487	338	Decreased 30.6%
Disciples seminarians	734	584	Decreased 20.4%

[1] Includes all categories of ministers engaged in full- or part-time ministries except students and retired ministers.

[2] Includes part-time and full-time pastors except retired pastors.

[3] Includes associate ministers, Christian education ministers, and ministers of music.

The data in table 1 contain some unavoidable inaccuracies due to the nature of the statistical records of the church. For example, the categories of participating members and congregations were instituted after 1961; thus, the 1961–71 comparative data are not precisely comparable. In addition, the *Year Book* office has estimated that during the mid-1960s, as the denomination began implementing restructure, about four hundred independent congregations requested that they be removed from the *Year Book*. This resulted in a statistical decline but not an actual loss to the denomination since these congregations had not functioned as cooperative and involved congregations for several years.

In some cases, congregations have not provided current reports for the *Year Book*. These congregations are included on the basis of estimates by regional ministers. Generally, estimated data are not as accurate as directly reported data.

However, even if these inaccuracies are taken into account, *the basic trend remains the same: decline in virtually every category of the dimensions of the church.* Perhaps the degree of decline is most accurately reflected in numbers of baptisms, which are based on written certificates (see table 2).

The data in table 2 report a steady decline in baptisms through the decade of the 1960s to 1972, during which 50% fewer baptisms were performed than in 1961.

TABLE 2
NUMBER OF BAPTISMS, 1961–72

Year	Baptisms	Decline Index
1961	46,479	100
1962	43,827	94
1963	40,183	89
1964	36,608	79
1965	34,966	75
1966	32,548	70
1967	30,442	65
1968	27,914	60
1969	26,460	57
1970	23,775	51
1971	24,218	52
1972	23,120	50

The black church. The above data describe a church that is predominantly white in its membership and professional ministry. The data in table 3 provide a comparative analysis of the predominantly white and predominantly black segments of the church.

Supply/demand needs for black leadership. An analysis of these data has led the Department of Ministry and Worship to estimate that a minimum of 102 black persons could be employed in full-time positions of professional church leadership during the next five years. Assuming sufficient income would be available to do so, this would create a need for 41 blacks to enter full-time ministry in the next five years. This estimate does not include any provision for predominantly white congregations or racially mixed congregations that may request black leadership.

In 1971—72, thirty black Disciples students were candidates for the ministry: six in seminary, twenty-four in undergraduate studies.

Contrasting styles of church life. A comparison of these data describing the predominantly white and predominantly black portions of the Christian Church reveals contrasting styles of church life and ministry. The white sector is comprised principally of congregations with 200—300 members that employ a full-time professional minister with a seminary degree. The black sector is comprised principally of congregations with fewer than 200 members that employ a part-time professional minister with no seminary education. The educational needs for these contrasting

TABLE 3

THE WHITE AND THE BLACK CHURCH CONTRASTED

Category of Analysis	Predominantly White	%	Predominantly Black	%
Number of congregations	3,347		548	
Average membership per congregation	226+		200−	
Ministers in standing	5,129		199	
Pastors of congregations	3,581	69.8	187	94.0
Number considered full-time	2,720	76.0	57	30.4
Educational Level of Professional Leadership				
Basic ministerial degree or equivalent	3,960	77.2	36	8.5
Master's degree or equivalent	610	11.9	18	4.2
College graduation	205	4.0	40	9.4
Some college study	226	4.4	85	20.0
High school graduation or less	133	2.6	246	57.9

NOTE: The data in this table must be considered estimates rather than precise measurements. They are based on a collection of statistics from a variety of sources, including the *1972 Year Book and Directory of the Christian Church (Disciples of Christ)*, a research study of 1,988 ministers conducted by the Pension Fund of the Christian Church (Disciples of Christ), and statistics on the black church compiled by the Department of Ministry and Worship of the Division of Homeland Ministries. Due to incomplete records, these data describing the black church are based on reliable estimates by black clergymen.

23

styles of church life and ministry would seem to contrast also and suggest differing methods for meeting these needs.

Supply and demand of ministers. Based on research conducted by the Pension Fund, the Department of Ministry and Worship, and the Board of Higher Education, from 1961 to 1971, *the Disciples have experienced a balance between supply/demand needs for full-time professional ministers in those positions which pay a "living wage."* There has not been sufficient collection and analysis of data to determine, at this time, whether the church is beginning to experience an oversupply of candidates for those positions. However, some attitudes and experiences of regional ministers suggest that this might be so.

The Disciples supply/demand experience differs markedly from those of the Episcopal Church, the United Methodist Church, and the United Presbyterian Church (U.S.A.), all of which have reported an oversupply of clergy in the last two years. It seems that the Disciples have experienced a relatively balanced decline in participating congregations, pastors of congregations, and seminarians, producing the balanced supply/demand situation. This decline has created serious problems for Disciples-related seminaries.

The Christian Church is undersupplied with full-time professional ministers for minority, rural, and small congregations. Based on the *1972 Year Book,* it appears that over one thousand Disciples congregations of these types do not have full-time pastors. This undersupply appears to be caused primarily by three factors: (1) the contrast between salary expectations of pastoral candidates and salary offers of these congregations; (2) the reluctance of many pastoral candidates to reside in non-urban/suburban settings; and (3) racial attitudes and life-styles that severely limit placement of white pastors with black congregations and vice versa.

Ministerial leadership for small, rural, and minority congregations is provided by a variety of persons, predominantly on a part-time and limited income basis:

1. Interim and/or retired ministers
2. Seminary or college faculty and students
3. Lay preachers—lay persons licensed by the church to perform limited ministerial duties
4. Bivocational ministers—ordained ministers who earn their living in another occupation
5. Pastors with multiple-church ministries—pastors serving two or more congregations of the same or different denominations

24

In some situations, full-time, professional ministerial leadership is provided by merging congregations of the same or different denominations or by financial subsidies from area or general church sources.

Data from regional ministers indicate that *there is a major need within the Christian Church for adequate supply of qualified ministers for small, rural, and minority congregations.* Failure to provide leadership for the congregations often results in the selection of ministers who may not cooperate with the objectives and mission of the corporate ministry of the Christian Church.

Church finance. An analysis of financial statistics (see table 4) shows that total monies for outreach and local congregation programs increased 37% from 1961 to 1971, 12% more than the rate of inflation during the same period. Outreach monies increased 27% from 1961 to 1966, but have remained at about the 1966 level since. Monies for local programs of congregations increased 39% from 1961 to 1971.

TABLE 4
CHURCH FINANCIAL STATISTICS

Year	Outreach[1]	Congregation	Total	Inflation Index[2]
1960−61	$13,834,129 (100)	$ 73,614,526 (100)	$ 87,448,655 (100)	100
1961−62	14,228,278 (103)	74,673,718 (101)	88,901,996 (102)	101
1962−63	15,491,436 (112)	78,596,247 (107)	94,087,683 (108)	102
1963−64	16,287,595 (118)	76,591,643 (104)	92,879,238 (106)	104
1964−65	16,925,770 (122)	89,337,324 (121)	106,263,094 (122)	105
1965−66	17,590,725 (127)	92,036,182 (125)	109,626,907 (125)	107
1966−67	17,509,072 (127)	93,733,093 (127)	111,242,165 (127)	110
1967−68	17,981,329 (130)	91,489,014 (124)	109,470,454 (125)	113
1968−69	18,158,245 (131)	98,075,065 (133)	116,233,310 (133)	116
1969−70	17,113,810 (124)	99,014,776 (135)	116,128,586 (133)	121
1970−71	17,560,559 (127)	102,492,293 (139)	120,052,852 (137)	125

[1] Contributions to concerns beyond local congregation.
[2] Computed from Consumer Price Index (all items).

The trend of church finance through the 1960s is clear: finances slightly higher than the rate of inflation. In fact, the rate of inflation increased most rapidly in 1969−70 and 1970−71, exceeding the rate of increase in all categories of church finance.

B. SUBJECTIVE DATA

Attitudes and opinions are important in the operation, success, or failure of any enterprise. In institutions such as churches, colleges, universities, and seminaries, feelings, attitudes, opinions, and convictions are critically important. Often they are the primary forces through which institutional objectives are realized or thwarted.

25

Literature search, personal observations of the life of the Christian Church, and analysis of a variety of interviews led the Study Commission to the hypothesis that considerable *divergence of attitude, opinion, and conviction* existed among various subgroups within the church, i.e., among types of laity and types of clergy. It was suspected that these attitudes congealed into differing expectations regarding some critical concerns of the church, for example, the purpose of the church and its ministry, the purpose and style of professional ministerial leadership, and the primary purposes of seminary education, all of which have great importance for ministerial education.

Louisville Assembly questionnaire. To examine systematically these expectations and their dimensions of difference, a questionnaire was designed that was administered widely at the Louisville Assembly in October, 1971, and later among seminaries and congregations. Total returns exceeded 2,000 responses. Of these, 1,640 have been divided into seven separate sample groups. They provide a spectrum of attitude and opinion broadly representative of the total denomination. These groups are described in table 5.

The results of this questionnaire revealed *broad theoretical agreement* among the seven groups regarding the call of laity and clergy to ministry and equal responsibility for the church's mission (range of 76% to 91%). Strong disagreement (range of 78% to 90%) was registered by all groups with the statement, "Basically, the church is not very different in its purpose from other social-service institutions in our society."

Although current literature suggests that there is widespread confusion and uncertainty among ministers regarding the role and purpose of their profession, none of the groups strongly agreed (18% to 31%) that this is a problem for most ministers. In addition, current literature suggests that

TABLE 5
RESPONDENTS TO LOUISVILLE ASSEMBLY QUESTIONNAIRE

Groups	Number	%
General ministers	56	18.2 % of all general ministers
Lay delegates to the assembly	472	17.9 % of all lay delegates
Local laity (not at assembly)	185	.02% of all participating members
Pastors of congregations	570	21.0 % of all full-time pastors
Seminary professors and administrators	45	50.0 % of all Disciples
Seminary students	50	10.1 % of all Disciples
Wives of ministers	262	about 5% of all wives of Disciples ministers

ministry has a low professional image and appeal. Yet a majority of all groups would encourage a member of their immediate families to enter the ministry (range 74% to 89%).

To assess perceptions of the relative importance of ministerial functions, respondents were asked to rank eight ministerial functions in the order of their importance. Table 6 describes the results.

TABLE 6
MINISTERIAL FUNCTIONS: PERCEIVED IMPORTANCE

Ministerial Functions	Average % of 1st Ranks Among Groups	Range of % of 1st Ranks Among Groups
Preaching and leading of worship services	25.4	10−48
Reading, study, sermon preparation	16.1	10−24
Pastoral visitation	13.1	5−20
Teaching and educational work with groups	12.0	2−21
Personal counseling	9.6	4−15
Administration of the program of the church	6.9	4−13
Denominational and ecumenical activities	.4	0− 1

It is striking that none of these functions received a first-rank choice any higher than 25.4%. Even preaching and leading worship services had a clear combined rank of first among only three groups: pastors, local laity, and seminary professors. However, denominational and ecumenical activities were ranked lowest by all groups. Involvement in community life and social problems was ranked low by all the groups with the exception of the seminarians, who ranked it first.

On many questionnaires, the respondents refused to rank these functions, or ranked them and complained about the difficulty or lack of validity in doing so. The point of most of the remarks was that it was virtually impossible to rank one function of ministry as more important than others. *All functions were seen as important and essential to effective ministry.*

To assess perceptions of the relative importance of purposes of the pastoral ministry, respondents were asked to rank five purposes in the order of their importance. Table 7 describes the results.

The data from tables 6 and 7 confirmed a growing impression among the members of the Study Commission, based on interviews and literature, that *one of the characteristic expectations and notions of ministry is the unity of various functions of ministry in the life-style of the professional*

TABLE 7
PURPOSES OF THE PASTORAL MINISTRY: PERCEIVED IMPORTANCE

Purposes of the Pastoral Ministry	Average % of 1st Ranks Among Groups	Range of % of 1st Ranks Among Groups
To proclaim the gospel with effectiveness and vitality	42.3	32−56
To lead and equip the congregation for its ministry to the larger society	32.3	18−48
To meet the spiritual and religious needs of the local congregation	14.9	4−28
To be a living example of moral and spiritual excellence	7.1	6− 9
To maintain and direct the various activities of the local congregation's program	1.3	0− 3

minister. Historically, Disciples have emphasized the preaching function. Now that seems to be combined with an emphasis on the equipping purpose of the pastoral ministry.

However, there is a very significant difference among the groups in perceived purposes of the pastoral ministry. Proclamation of the gospel and equipping the congregation received either the highest or second highest percentage of first ranks from all groups, *except the local laity.* Forty-two percent of them ranked proclamation first, *28% ranked meeting spiritual and religious needs of the local congregation first,* and 18% ranked equipping the congregation first. To illustrate the point a different way, an average of only 8.5% of the four "professional ministerial" groups—pastors, general ministers, seminary professors/administrators, and seminary students—ranked meeting spiritual and religious needs of the congregation as first, while an average of 23.3% of the laity groups ranked meeting these needs as first.

A series of questions asking respondents to compare new ministers and their predecessors revealed an image of new ministers as (1) better prepared intellectually, (2) having a greater sense of obligation to the surrounding community, (3) but not as well prepared spiritually. A majority of general ministers (57%) and local laity (57%) perceived new ministers as more concerned with salary and fringe benefits.

Graduate seminary education was recognized among all groups as necessary for an adequately prepared and competent pastoral ministry (range: 65% to 93%; average: 82.0%). Even though all groups basically disagreed with the statement, "Our denominational seminaries are weakening the faith and commitment of ministerial students" (range: 36% to 82%; average: 61.6%), the uncertainty of lay delegates (41%) and of local laity (41%) suggested that they were uneasy about this issue.

Perception of expected goals of theological education were assessed by asking respondents to rank eight goals in order of importance. Table 8 summarizes the responses.

TABLE 8
GOALS OF THEOLOGICAL EDUCATION: PERCEIVED IMPORTANCE

Goals of Theological Education	Average % of 1st Ranks Among Groups	Range of % of 1st Ranks Among Groups
1. To deepen the Christian commitment of students and strengthen their moral and spiritual life	28.3	11−48
2. To aid students in being more sensitive to the feelings, needs, and attitudes of people	14.0	7−28
3. To train students in the professional skills for the ministries of the church	12.3	5−16
4. To aid students in realizing their own personal (human) growth	12.3	5−22
5. To train students to think theologically and critically	12.0	2−33
6. To transmit to students the intellectual heritage and knowledge of the Christian faith	11.6	6−15
7. To teach students to be continuing lifelong learners	6.0	2− 9
8. To train students to be agents of social change	3.4	0−13

An analysis of percentages of respondents from each group that ranked various goals as the most important for theological education provides some illuminating contrasts. (See table 9.)

The data in table 9 suggest that *pastors, general ministers, and laity believe the major goal of theological education is moral and spiritual development while seminary professors/administrators and students do not.* In fact, 33% of the seminary professors/administrators believe training students to think theologically and critically is the major goal, while 28% of seminary students believe the major goal is to aid students in being more sensitive to the feelings, needs, and attitudes of people.

It is likely that two separate issues are mixed together in these responses: (1) qualities that ministers ought to have (Christian commitment, a strong

TABLE 9
GOALS OF THEOLOGICAL EDUCATION:
CONTRASTS IN PERCEIVED IMPORTANCE

Groups	Goal #1	Goal #2	Goal #5
Local laity	48%	9%	2%
Lay delegates	44%	10%	5%
Clergy wives	36%	19%	4%
General ministers	25%	11%	21%
Pastors of congregations	22%	14%	9%
Seminary students	12%	28%	10%
Seminary professors and administrators	11%	7%	33%

moral and spiritual life, sensitivity to others) and (2) the role and responsibility of the seminary in developing these qualities. For example, is it reasonable to expect seminaries to be the principal element in forming the moral and spiritual character of adult students? Is it not also the responsibility of the home, the congregation, and the undergraduate college?

The greatest divergences of attitude and expectation seem to exist between seminary students and local laity regarding style of church life and ministerial leadership, particularly as these relate to social issues. Some selected data illustrate these different attitudes. (See table 10.)

Differing and unrealistic expectations. The data in table 10 compare attitudes and expectations and illustrate that differences of degree rather than complete opposition are most common. These and other data from interviews and literature have led the commission to the finding that *there are significant differences in expectation regarding a wide spectrum of church life and style of ministerial leadership between laity and pastoral ministers. These differing expectations often lead to unrealistic expectations on the part of both parties, often producing mutual disappointment, distress, unhealthy conflict, and debilitation of the life of the congregation.* For example, Mills and Koval found that the major form of stress for the Protestant clergy is in the area of personal or ideological conflict with parishioners.[1]

The dimensions of these differing expectations are many and varied. Reference to some might be useful as generalizations *which may not always be accurate in every circumstance.*

1. PROFESSIONAL ROLE. Ministers tend to view their role as leading and equipping the laity for their ministry to the world. Laity tend to view the minister as *their chaplain,* employed to preach, teach, and

1. Edgar W. Mills and John P. Koval, *Stress in the Ministry* (Washington, D.C.: Ministry Studies Board, 1971).

TABLE 10
CONTRASTING ATTITUDES OF LOCAL LAITY AND DISCIPLES SEMINARIANS

	Local Laity			Seminarians		
	Agree	Uncertain	Disagree	Agree	Uncertain	Disagree
The primary task of the church is to live the Christian life among its own membership rather than to try to change society.	20%	22%	57%	2%	26%	72%
The church should be a place of refuge and quiet reflection, uninvolved with social and political events.	23%	21%	56%	0%	4%	96%
The church must become increasingly involved in meeting and influencing power structures of our society.	60%	18%	22%	80%	18%	2%
It is appropriate for ministers to participate in acts of civil protest.	22%	28%	50%	74%	16%	10%
Our denomination should increase its support of special ministries, such as those to college campuses, high-rise apartments, migrant workers, drug addicts.	38%	36%	23%	90%	10%	0%
In recent years the church has not given sufficient emphasis to winning persons for Christ.	61%	26%	13%	36%	40%	24%
While ministers are faced with problems and irritations in their work, the number and seriousness of these are probably no greater than in other professions.	52%	18%	29%	22%	38%	40%

comfort them. Jeffrey K. Hadden, a sociologist, made similar findings in his studies of Protestant laity and clergy.[2]

2. PROFESSIONAL OR HIRELING? Ministers tend to view themselves as professionals who function as skilled leaders according to objectives and standards determined by the profession. In addition, they tend to view themselves in relation to their professional peers, their denomination, and the Church Universal. Laity tend to view the

2. *The Gathering Storm in the Churches* (Garden City, N.Y.: Doubleday & Company, 1969).

minister as their employee, hired to accomplish the objectives of the congregation.[3]

3. SALARY. Ministers desire and often expect a salary more nearly commensurate with professionals of comparable education and status. Congregations generally expect to pay ministers salaries considerably below income levels of comparable professionals. For example, in 1971 the average "asking" salary of ministers seeking relocation exceeded the average offering salary of available positions by more than $1,300 per year. In 1971 the average annual compensation for all Disciples ministers was approximately $7,000 plus parsonage. In 1970 the average starting offer for a college graduate in business administration with four years of college (B.A. degree) was $8,604. Candidates with five to six years of college (M.A. degree) received an average of $12,528. Many graduating Disciples seminarians in 1971 suggested that an annual $10,000 salary be guaranteed by the Christian Church.[4]

4. LIFE-STYLE. Graduating seminarians, through seven or eight years of undergraduate and graduate study, tend to develop a scholarly life-style oriented toward study, critical analysis, formal papers, and interpersonal relations within the academic community. They bring this developed life-style with them to their first years of ministry. In contrast, laity tend to expect an interpersonally warm pastor who communicates in terms and styles that "average" laity can appreciate and understand; a pastor whose education is evident but not esoteric. They appear to want ministerial education that implements the objectives of the congregation without radically questioning and disturbing its life-style.

5. RELATIONSHIP OF PASTOR TO CONGREGATION. Depending on the nature of their previous experiences, ministers tend to view the congregation as a community of persons who will give them personal support, appreciation, and understanding. This may be particularly true of seminarians whose expectations of their first years of ministry are based on their experiences as popular youth leaders and fair-haired youth of the congregation. Laity tend to expect ministers to be secure and strong and to have little need for support and ministering from the congregation.

6. AUTHORITY AND LEADERSHIP. Ministers expect to have

3. William Martin Smith, *Servants Without Hire* (Nashville: Disciples of Christ Historical Society, 1968).

4. These data are taken from a variety of reports by the Board of Higher Education, the Department of Ministry and Worship, and the Pension Fund.

considerable impact on the life and program of a congregation. They hope to implement new and creative ideas and tend to think of "their ministry" in those terms. Laity tend to view the church plant and the program of the congregation as "their church" and often feel that any noticeable change must be congruent with their notions of what "their church" is. If either party finds its expectations denied or thwarted, identity and authority crises often occur.

C. THE CHURCH IN CRISIS

The Christian Church, like most other American main-line churches today, is undergoing a crisis of significant proportions. The symptoms of the crisis are decreasing institutional strength (members, money, professional ministers) and damaging conflict among clergy and laity regarding authority, purpose, and style of ministry.

Martin E. Marty, professor and administrator at the Divinity School of the University of Chicago and sage observer of American religious life, suggests four continuing trends in the life of American main-line churches:

1. Continuing, moderate decline of institutional strength with eventual stabilization, probably in the late 1970s.
2. Continuing economic pressures that will take their toll in reduced national church bureaucracies.
3. Increasing localism. "When people do get together, most of their energies are going to be focused on how they can keep their own show going."
4. Increase of the bivocational model of professional ministry: not the man of secular employment who becomes a lay preacher, but the professional minister who can take on some secular employment.[5]

The effects of the above trends are being felt in the ecumenical movement also. The World Council of Churches, the National Council of Churches, and the Consultation on Church Union are undergoing attack and criticism from some of the local constituency of the participating denominations and churches. However, ecumenism among congregations and other local institutions, in a variety of consortia and cooperative forms, appears to be increasing.

Beyond survival. Virtually every American main-line church is undergoing major restructure of organizational and governance patterns. However, organizational survival, per se, does not appear to be the real issue. By selective retrenchment—i.e., reduced budgets, programs, and

5. Personal interview, January, 1972

personnel—main-line denominations probably can survive the 1970s. *The real issue is planning change for a more effective corporate ministry during a time of organizational adversity.*

If the Christian Church is to survive the 1970s with sufficient capacity for effective ministry to the world in the remainder of this century, it must develop radical strategies, that is, plans and programs that seek to resolve the root problems which have caused its malaise.

It is the Study Commission's judgment that *the effectiveness of the corporate ministry of the Christian Church (Disciples of Christ) is primarily dependent on the adequacy and effectiveness of congregations, which in turn depend on the quality of their leadership—both lay and clergy.*

The key person in the development and maintenance of effective ministry by congregations is the pastoral minister. His or her principal function is to equip the congregation, corporately and individually, for its ministry to the larger society. That equipping task, by its nature and under the current state of the church and society, is broad and demanding, requiring unique personal qualities and professional skills.

Under the best circumstances, the development and education of effective church leadership is a complex and difficult task. When the current problems facing the church are considered—e.g., finance; lay/clergy conflict; needs for specialized, bivocational and lay-professional ministers—the development and education of laity and clergy who can function effectively within these constraints seem almost impossible to achieve.

Priority of leadership development. Therefore, *unless the Christian Church makes leadership development its first priority in the immediate years ahead, providing increased and creative financial and program support, it is doubtful that professional and lay leadership of sufficient effectiveness to renew the church in the 1980s and 1990s will be developed.*

3

Ministry
as a Profession

Professional status of the ministry. Although the ministry is one of the historic professions in addition to law and medicine, the current status of the ministry among the professions is ambiguous. There is resistance within the church to classifying ministry as a profession. Some feel it treats ministry as just another job, not as a special calling. Others feel it denigrates the layman, giving him the status of "amateur" as distinct from "professional." Another source of ambiguity is the absence of a commonly accepted definition of what a professional is.

Nevertheless, there are common aspects of the work and life-style of recognized professions. These provide a rough measure of professionalization, a process of change within occupations and professions toward clearer and more complete expression of professionalism.

Table 11 compares some characteristics of professionals with characteristics of those in the pastoral ministry, the major form of ministry in the Christian Church (Disciples of Christ).

Role of professional associations. A highly developed professional association usually establishes:

1. A code of ethics for the profession
2. Criteria of admission to the profession, including educational standards
3. Formal methods of examining and certifying professional competence
4. Career lines within the profession

5. Continuing education for upgrading the profession
6. An ethos of its own that enables the individual practitioner to feel a deep and lifelong commitment to the practices and life-styles of the profession and provides support services to that end

Professionalization tends to produce professional associations which provide their members with psychological and social roots amid a changing society, for example, a common sense of identity, self-regulation, lifetime membership, shared values, a common language, and strong socialization of new members.

TABLE 11
PROFESSIONAL CHARACTERISTICS OF THE PASTORAL MINISTRY

Characteristics of a Professional	Characteristics of a Pastoral Minister
1. Possesses specialized body of knowledge	Possesses knowledge of theological, historical, and biblical fields
2. Possesses specialized skills	Possesses ministerial skills (preaching, teaching, counseling, administration, leadership of worship)
3. Has completed a prolonged period of education and training	Has completed 4 years of college and 3 years of seminary including supervised field work
4. Makes decisions based on general principles and knowledge rather than established routine	Makes decisions based on understanding of the Christian faith and its application to particular circumstances
5. Joins or establishes associations of professional peers who assume primary responsibility for developing, directing, and maintaining the profession, rather than the employer or client	May be a member of the Academy of Parish Clergy, the Society for the Advancement of Continuing Education for Ministry (SACEM), or an informal, local support/professional group

NOTE: This table gives a composite of characteristics suggested by several authors, e.g., Glasse, *Profession: Minister*; Shein, *Education for the Professions*.

Increasing professionalization of the ministry. On the basis of the above characteristics, it seems clear that the pastoral ministry can be classified as a profession that is not highly professionalized at the present time. The principal agents of professionalization are professional associations. The recent creation of SACEM (1968) and the Academy of Parish Clergy (1969) suggests that an important trend is the increasing professionalization of the pastoral ministry. This trend will probably have significant impact on future styles of pastoral ministry, other forms of ministry, and education for them.

From authoritarianism to collegiality. Historically, the pastoral minister in America has been a loner, operating independently from other clergy, dependent primarily on his own skills, energy, understanding, and capacity to establish authority for his ministry among the members of his congregation. This style has tended to develop an authoritarian professional who is threatened by loss of authority to lay members, associate ministers, regional ministers, and others. Need for members of the congregation to perceive the pastor as "my minister" has augmented this authoritarian style. Generally, efforts to create harmonious and effective multiple ministries for congregations have been marked with frustration and failure.

The Academy of Parish Clergy seeks a new professional style of ministry, *collegiality*. The academy suggests that the minister explore a variety of methods to establish ecumenical collaboration, accountability, and continuing education among professional peers. Reflecting the shared responsibility among clergy and laity for the ministry of the church to the world, the academy also seeks collegiality and teamwork with lay persons, engaging them in planning, action-reflection education, evaluation of program in ministry, etc.

Assuming that a collegial style of ministry becomes dominant in the future, the implications for the personal and professional qualifications necessary for the equipping function of ministry are considerable.

Requisite personal qualities for the pastoral ministry. Some of these personal qualities are:

1. Faith in Jesus Christ and commitment to a life of Christian discipleship
2. Definite and informed decision, in response to God, to serve in the order of ministry
3. High intelligence
4. High energy and good health
5. Human warmth
6. Trust in other persons and willingness to share responsibility and authority
7. Intrapersonal security
8. Capacity for the development of professional ministerial skills

Requisite skills for the pastoral ministry. The Academy of Parish Clergy has identified competencies required for effective parish ministry.

To do his work in the parish a pastor must develop basic skills in each of the five areas demanding his professional competence: (1) responding to his particular situation, (2) managing his parish organization, (3) relating to individuals, (4) developing his own personal and professional resources and (5) planning and providing for public worship.

1. Competence in relating effectively to congregations in their particular social, economic, political, and cultural context demands situational skills that do not necessarily transfer from one context to another:
   a. skills in communicating, e.g. preaching and writing.
   b. skills in interpreting the religious heritages to contemporary life.
   c. skills in interpreting life issues in terms of both inherited and emerging religious symbols.
   d. skills in understanding and providing for the social, recreational, and amusement life of the church.
   e. skills in helping the congregation to effect change in its community.
2. Competence in the management of religious organizations requires the following skills:
   a. skills in effective participation in and leadership of groups.
   b. skills in assistance to a religious organization in identifying and achieving its goals.
   c. skills in recruitment of persons for the organization and for jobs within the organization.
   d. skills in management functions, e.g. planning, organizing, directing and evaluating.
   e. skills in supervision within the voluntary organization.
   f. skills in sociological and political analysis of the congregation and the communities to which it is related.
   g. skills in creative handling of conflict.
   h. skills in money and property management.
3. Competence in helping individuals to acquire maturity, health, and strength requires these skills:
   a. skills in teaching.
   b. skills in leading people in their personal spiritual lives.
   c. skills in counseling and referrals.
   d. skills in responding effectively to people's expectations of his role.
4. Competence in developing his own personal and professional resources involves the following skills:
   a. skills in using the case study method, e.g., action-reflection.
   b. skills in developing the inner-life, e.g., prayer and meditation.
   c. skills in confronting his own beliefs, convictions, and doubts in the light of heritage.
   d. skills in identifying a need for professional assistance and making use of consultative services.
   e. skills in making use of opportunities for career development and continuing education.
   f. skills in dealing with his own expectations of himself.

5. Competence in developing and leading public worship necessitates the use of nearly all the skills identified in the other four areas.[1]

Political skills in the ministry. As noted above, the Christian Church is an organization characterized by the voluntary association of members and groups, lay control, aversion to clerical or hierarchical authority, and a corporate ministry dependent on the maintenance of a spirit of cooperation and consensus. All of these factors require "political skills" for effective ministry and that requirement runs throughout the whole structure of the denomination and all forms of ministry. "Political skills" in this context means the ability to establish a constituency of support and trust among the members of the congregation in addition to shaping and reshaping consensus among the membership.

James Gustafson has articulated this concept of pastoral leadership most clearly.

The pastor of a local church must effectively win the political support of the voting members of a congregation to be called to the office of pastor. . . . He must meet the expectations of the congregation to remain in office, but he must meet the expectations of his religious convictions by changing the character of the congregation in light of his religious purposes. . . .

The pattern is more comparable to that of a congressman from a conservative district who is interested in progressive reforms than it is to the local attorney or the physician. . . .

He is responsive to the consensus that exists in his constituency—he must be, to maintain himself in office—but he also seeks to reshape that consensus through his persuasive powers. He seeks to direct it into greater conformity to the central religious and moral convictions that are the church's and also presumably his own. His effectiveness is judged not merely by his tenure in office but by his success in redirecting the consensus. . . .

Consensus formation is always in process, not only because unanimity can never be achieved but also because the vitality of the religious group is maintained as it seeks to come to a more or less common mind on the essentials of the faith and on the activities it ought to engage in. This means that the function of giving leadership to this process is not occasionally, but always, at the center of the task of the clergyman.[2]

Within the Christian Church the office of pastoral minister, as office, contains little formative power today. The capacity for influence and

1. *The Journal of The Academy of Parish Clergy* (April, 1971), pp. 63—64. Copyright 1971, Academy of Parish Clergy. Used by permission. This material was revised and published by the Academy in 1972 under the title "Competence in the Parish Ministry."

2. Gustafson, James, "Political Images of the Ministry," *The Church, the University, and Social Policy* by Kenneth Underwood *et al.* The Danforth Study of Campus Ministries. (Middletown, Conn.: Wesleyan University Press, 1969), II, pp. 252, 254, 256. Used by permission of the publisher.

change lies in the interrelationship of trust and support between pastor and people. This interrelationship must be established *before* major reshaping of consensus is functionally possible. Trust and support appear to be established through the competent and loving practice of the historic functions of ministry within a setting that often contains considerable philosophical conflict between pastor and people.

Leadership talent of the dimensions and qualities required for effective ministry is available within the rich pluralism of the American society. *Persons of diverse cultural, ethnic, racial, and economic backgrounds with leadership talents and qualities must be identified, nurtured, guided, challenged, educated, and supported if the Christian Church (Disciples of Christ) is to have an effective professional ministry.*

4

Development of a Professional Ministry for the Christian Church

The process of ministerial development. In the Christian Church professional ministers are developed through a complex process that involves, at one point or another in the process, all manifestations of the church and its related educational institutions. Generally, the process has four stages: (1) interpretation of the profession of ministry; (2) recruitment, enlistment, nurture, and education for ministry; (3) certification and ordination for ministry; and (4) career development in ministry. This chapter presents a description of the programs and processes that generally fall under these stages of ministerial development.

Description of stages. *To interpret the ministry* means to assist persons in understanding the ministry, its functions, and its viability as a career so that they might view it in relation to their interests and talents. Interpretation includes involvement in church life, participation in leadership roles, assumption of ministerial duties on occasion, etc.

Recruitment for ministry is the direct attempt to promote the interest and commitment of an individual to ministry as a career. *Enlistment for ministry* is that point where a person formally indicates his intention to prepare for ministry as his profession. Interpretation, recruitment, and enlistment for ministry are aspects of God's call to ministry through the church and the person's response to that call. *Nurture and education* for ministry refers primarily to the totality of relationships and educational experiences that a candidate is provided to prepare him for the profession of ministry.

Certification for ministry refers to processes of ordination and induction into ministerial standing of the church following completion of formal education.

Career development in ministry refers to the variety of ways the church aids the minister in the practice of his profession, including professional placement, continuing education, professional and personal guidance, health care, retirement, and emergency benefits.

The process of ministerial development in the Christian Church is not immediately obvious, principally because it is a complex process and there is no single unit of the church that coordinates or administers the process. It is a montage of individual efforts by a variety of structures within the church. An exhaustive analysis of all aspects of this process is beyond the scope of this report, but perhaps reference to some programs will illustrate the nature of this complex process.

Interpretation of the ministry by the congregation. Attitudes regarding the profession of ministry are shaped first within the congregation. Interpretation of ministry, formal and informal, is made through experiences of the family and the congregation. Most studies of career influence for ministry indicate that the pastor of the congregation is the principal catalyst which informs and attracts or repels persons to ministry. However, interviews confirm the impression that the total context of congregational and family attitudes regarding the ministry as a profession is also a critical influence. Positive images and attitudes among congregations which portray the ministry as an important, worthwhile, and fulfilling profession are essential to the development of a qualified and effective professional ministry.

One model for interpretation of and introduction to the ministry by a congregation is a program conducted by the Peachtree Christian Church of Atlanta, Georgia. Each summer it gives several undergraduate college students a view of the varieties of professional ministry in that area, with additional opportunities for discussion, action-reflection, and trying themselves out in one or more of the ministerial functions. Over the years, this program has made a significant contribution to ministerial leadership in the Christian Church.

A program of this type is beyond the resources of many congregations. However, wide involvement of pastors and lay leaders in programs of interpreting ministry to youth groups in the congregation and the surrounding community, would be most useful.

Churchwide programs of ministerial interpretation. Several programs to interpret ministry as a career, conducted by general units of the church, are noteworthy. In cooperation with various regions, the Department of Ministry and Worship employs and supervises three to five seminarians for the *Person to Person Interpretation Program* (PPIP), interpretation of ministry to high school-age young people, primarily through summer conferences. The Board of Higher Education provides ten to fifteen predominantly minority, college-age young people with *Short Term Employment Experiences in Ministry* (STEEM). The objective of this program is to provide students undecided in their career aspirations with opportunities to discover and validate an interest in church occupations. Each spring, the Board of Higher Education administers a *Senior Seminarian Conference on the Ministry,* sponsored by the church and designed to promote reflection on ministry in the Christian Church. In addition, these units cooperatively sponsor student conferences on the ministry and liaison support of the Commission on Vocation and Enlistment of the National Council of Churches.

A. RELATED UNDERGRADUATE EDUCATIONAL INSTITUTIONS

College years are a critical time for persons to consider career options. Faculty, administrators, and students are influential in a career decision. Primary interpreters of ministry on campus are the campus ministers, religion faculty, student peers, and pastors of congregations closely related to the campus. They are also the principal campus agents for the recruitment, enlistment, nurture, and education of professional ministers.

Through the Board of Higher Education there are twenty-three colleges, universities, and schools of religion related to the Christian Church which provide undergraduate education. From 1961 to 1972, the alumni of these institutions comprised 57% of all Disciples seminarians.[1] Obviously, the contribution of these institutions to the development of a professional ministry for the church is crucial. Therefore, a study of ministerial education must include some analysis of these institutions and their programs of ministerial development and education.

Related colleges. Table 12 provides a capsule description of the twenty-three institutions and programs of higher education related to the Christian Church through membership in the Board of Higher Education.

There are fourteen related colleges. Ten are four-year liberal arts colleges offering a variety of baccalaureate degrees and preprofessional curricula. One is a two-year liberal arts college offering the Associate in Arts degree. Two are five-year liberal arts colleges offering the bachelor's and master's degrees. Northwest Christian College is a specialized institution, offering the degrees of Bachelor of Arts, Bachelor of Science, and Bachelor of Theology, and a curriculum which gives major emphasis to

---

1. This figure is slightly inaccurate. Students who received their preseminary education through one of the Disciples schools of religion affiliated with state universities are not included in this figure. Their inclusion might increase this figure by 1 to 2%.

TABLE 12
Description of Institutions and Programs of Higher Education Related to the Christian Church

Name and Location of Institutions	Founding Date	Type of Institution	Degrees Granted	Total Enrollment (Full-time Students, Fall, 1970)	Disciples	Undergraduate Ministerial Students	1970–71 Operating Expenses (in Thousands of Dollars)
Colleges							
Atlantic Christian College Wilson, North Carolina	1902	Coed, 4-year Liberal Arts	Variety of bachelor's degrees	1,558	193	22	$2,931
Bethany College Bethany, West Virginia	1840	Coed, 4-year Liberal Arts	Bachelor of Arts Bachelor of Science	1,075	94	30	3,775
Chapman College Orange, California	1861	Coed, 5-year Liberal Arts Graduate/Professional	Bachelor of Arts Bachelor of Music Variety of master's degrees	2,319[1]	382	67	6,523
Columbia College Columbia, Missouri	1851	Coed, 4-year Liberal Arts	Associate in Arts Bachelor of Arts	492	51	—	1,903
Culver-Stockton College Canton, Missouri	1853	Coed, 4-year Liberal Arts	Variety of bachelor's degrees	736	147	15	2,098
Eureka College Eureka, Illinois	1848	Coed, 4-year Liberal Arts	Bachelor of Arts Bachelor of Science	487	75	23	1,473[2]
Hiram College Hiram, Ohio	1850	Coed, 4-year Liberal Arts	Bachelor of Arts	1,164	120	18	3,535
Jarvis Christian College Hawkins, Texas	1910	Coed, Predominantly Black, 4-year Liberal Arts	Variety of bachelor's degrees	707	44	7	2,059
Lynchburg College Lynchburg, Virginia	1903	Coed, 5-year Liberal Arts Graduate/Professional	Bachelor of Arts Bachelor of Science Variety of master's degrees	1,804	122	20	4,490

Institution	Founded	Type	Degrees	Enrollment			
Midway College, Midway, Kentucky	1847	Women, 2-year Liberal Arts	Associate in Arts, Associate Degree in Nursing	190	48	—	676
Northwest Christian College, Eugene, Oregon	1895	Coed, 4-year Professional and Liberal Arts	Variety of bachelor's degrees	343	303	165	677
Tougaloo College, Tougaloo, Mississippi	1871	Coed, Predominantly Black, 4-year Liberal Arts	Bachelor of Arts, Bachelor of Science	730	?	—	3,071
Transylvania University, Lexington, Kentucky	1780[3]	Coed, 4-year Liberal Arts	Bachelor of Arts	855	190	31	2,899
William Woods College, Fulton, Missouri	1890	Women, 4-year Liberal Arts	Bachelor of Arts, Bachelor of Science	850	?	—	2,968
TOTALS				13,310	1,769	398	$39,078
Universities							
Butler University, Indianapolis, Indiana	1855	Coed, 5-year Liberal Arts Graduate/Professional	Variety of bachelor's and master's degrees	2,752[1]	?	9	$ 6,861
Drake University, Des Moines, Iowa	1881	Coed, 5-year Liberal Arts Graduate/Professional	Variety of bachelor's, master's, and doctor's degrees	5,563[1]	161	23	14,915
Phillips University, Enid, Oklahoma	1906	Coed, 5-year Liberal Arts Graduate/Professional Incl. Seminary	Variety of bachelor's and master's degrees, Doctor of Ministry	1,149[1]	543	149	2,527 (incl. seminary)
Texas Christian University, Fort Worth, Texas	1873	Coed, Liberal Arts Graduate/Professional Incl. Seminary	Variety of bachelor's and master's degrees, Doctor of Ministry, Doctor of Philosophy	5,118[1]	824	110	15,246 (incl. seminary)
TOTALS				14,582	1,528	291	$39,549

Continued on following page

TABLE 12—*Continued*

Name and Location of Institutions	Founding Date	Type of Institution	Degrees Granted	Total Enrollment (Full-time Students, Fall, 1970)	Disciples	Undergraduate Ministerial Students	1970-71 Operating Expenses (in Thousands of Dollars)
Bible Chairs and Schools of Religion							
Christian College of Georgia Athens, Georgia	1946	Instruction in religion Preministerial and lay theological education	Degrees granted by University of Georgia	42[2]	23[2]	7[2]	$ 66
Cotner College Lincoln, Nebraska	1889	Instruction in religion Preministerial education	Degrees granted by University of Nebraska	145	12	26	68
Drury School of Religion Springfield, Missouri	1909	Instruction in religion and philosophy	Degrees granted by Drury College	486	105	34	50
Kansas Bible Chair Lawrence, Kansas	1901	Instruction in religion	Degrees granted by University of Kansas	1,000	?	?	22
Missouri School of Religion Columbia, Missouri	1895	Instruction in religion Graduate Seminary	Undergraduate degrees granted by University of Missouri Variety of master's degrees at graduate level	233	?	?	190 (incl. seminary)
TOTALS				1,906			$396

[1] Full-time equivalent.
[2] 1969–70 figure.
[3] Related to Christian Church in 1865.

courses in Bible, religion, church music, and other subjects for church workers, lay and professional.

Most of these colleges have predominantly white, coeducational student bodies. Jarvis Christian College and Tougaloo College have predominantly black student bodies. Midway College, William Woods College, and Columbia College have predominantly female student bodies. All institutions are fully accredited by the appropriate nationally recognized institutional accrediting association.

Enrollment. The total full-time enrollment of these fourteen colleges in the fall of 1970 was 13,310 students (range 190 to 2,319; average 951). There were 1,769 Disciples students enrolled in the twelve institutions reporting this statistic (Tougaloo College and William Woods College excluded), comprising 15.1% of the total enrollment (range 7.0% to 88.3%). Of the total enrollment, 398, or 3.0%, were ministerial students (range: 7 to 651; average: 28). Of these, 286, or 72%, were Disciples.

Finances. The total operating expenses of these fourteen colleges for 1970—71 were $39,079,000 (range: $676,000 to $6,523,000; average: $2,791,286). Through Unified Promotion and designated church contributions, the Christian Church contributed $875,817 in 1970—71 toward the operating expenses of these colleges (range: $8,139 to $135,-843; average: $62,558). *That amount was 2.2% of the total operating expenses of these colleges (range: 0.3% to 20.0%).*

Related universities. There are four related universities. All of them provide liberal arts and graduate/professional instruction and offer a variety of bachelor's and master's degrees. Texas Christian University and Phillips University have graduate seminaries offering a variety of master's degrees and the Doctor of Ministry degree for the professional ministries of the Church Universal. Only Texas Christian University offers the Doctor of Philosophy degree. Drake University offers doctorates in education and the arts of teaching. All universities are fully accredited.

The total full-time equivalent enrollment of these institutions in the fall of 1970 was 14,582 students (range: 1,149 to 5,563; average: 3,646). There were 1,528 Disciples students enrolled in the three universities reporting this statistic (Butler excluded), comprising 12.9% of the total enrollment (range: 2.9% to 47.3%). *Of the total enrollment, 291, or 2.0%, were undergraduate ministerial students (range: 9 to 149; average: 73). Of these, 151, or 52%, were Disciples.*

The total operating expenses of these universities for 1970-71 were $39,-549,000 (range: $2,527,000 to $15,246,000; average: $9,887,338). Through Unified Promotion and designated church contributions, the Christian Church contributed $503,236 in 1970—71 toward the operating expenses of Texas Christian University and Phillips University.[2] *That amount was 1.3% of the total operating expenses of the four universities.* Butler University and Drake University receive no contributions from the Christian Church through Unified Promotion.

Related Bible chairs and schools of religion. There are five related Bible chairs and schools of religion. All of them offer instruction in religion as an academic subject for credit in affiliated institutions of higher education. Four of them are related to state universities; Drury School of Religion is related to Drury College, a private institution affiliated with the United Church of Christ. In addition, all of them offer some instruction, guidance, and nurture of undergraduate ministerial students. In 1970–71, Missouri School of Religion provided a graduate seminary program. It has been phased out, as of 1972–73, in order that the total resources of the institution might be focused on its undergraduate program.

In the fall of 1970, a total of 1,906 students received instruction in religion through these programs (range: 42 to 1,000; average: 381). An accurate count of Disciples or undergraduate ministerial students in these programs could not be made because two of them did not report this statistic.

The total operating expenses of these Bible chairs and schools of religion in 1970–71 were $387,787 (range: $21,824 to $189,772; average: $77,557).[3] Through Unified Promotion and designated church contributions, the Christian Church contributed $124,046 to the operating expenses of these programs (range: $14,146 to $38,757; average: $24,809). That amount was 32.0% of the total operating expenses of these programs (range: 20.4% to 64.8%).

Changes in enrollment and finance patterns of these institutions during the 1960s are provided in table 13.

Colleges. During the 1960s, among the related colleges, *total enrollment increased 77% while the number of ministerial students decreased 51%.* Operating expenses increased 266% while church contributions increased 58%, reducing the ratio of support by the church from 5.2% to 2.2% of the total operating expenditures of the related colleges.

Universities. Among the related universities, *enrollment increased 7% while the number of ministerial students decreased 51%.* Total operating expenses increased 154% while church contributions increased 15%, reducing the ratio of church support from 3.2% to 1.3% of the total operating expenditures of the related universities.

2. Includes contributions to seminaries.
3. Graduate seminary programs are included in these statistics when they are part of the institution.

TABLE 13
Related Institutions of Higher Education: Comparative Statistics

CATEGORY OF ANALYSIS	COLLEGES (14 Institutions) Fiscal Year			UNIVERSITIES (4 Institutions) Fiscal Year			SCHOOLS OF RELIGION Fiscal Year		
	1960–61	1970–71	% of Change	1960–61	1970–71	% of Change	1960–61	1970–71	% of Change
Total enrollment	7,505	13,310	+77	13,600	14,582	+7	1,675	1,906	+14
Average enrollment per institution	536	951		3,400	3,646		335	381	
Ministerial students (undergraduate)	816	398	−51	588	291	−51			
Operating expenses (in thousands of dollars)	$10,670	$39,079	+266	$15,568	$39,549	+154	$ 201	$ 396	+197
Church contributions to operating expenses (in thousands of dollars)	$ 555	$ 876	+58	$ 494	$ 503	+15	$ 75	$ 129	+172
% of operating expenses	5.2	2.2		3.2	1.3		37.3	32.0	
Total operating surplus/deficit[1]	−$35,417	−$441,104		+$364,968	−$231,348		−$7,885	−$68,679	

[1] This figure is an annual deficit, not an accumulative deficit.

Schools of religion. Among the Bible chairs and schools of religion, *total enrollment increased 14%.* The number of ministerial students is unknown. Operating expenses increased 197% while church contributions increased 172%, reducing the ratio of church support from 48.2% to 32.0%.

Increasing deficits. Comparison of 1960−61 and 1970−71 operating surplus/deficit figures shows considerable increase of operating deficits among all three types of institutions. Obviously, *these institutions are undergoing a financial crunch of significant proportions, which seems to be caused primarily by rapidly escalating expenses.* Table 14 shows relative changes that occurred in sources of operating income during the 1960s as these institutions strove to maintain financial solvency.

TABLE 14

RELATED INSTITUTIONS OF HIGHER EDUCATION: SOURCES OF OPERATING INCOME

CATEGORY OF ANALYSIS	COLLEGES (13 Institutions)		UNIVERSITIES (3 Institutions)		SCHOOLS OF RELIGION (5 Institutions)	
	Fiscal Year		Fiscal Year		Fiscal Year	
	1960−61	1969−70	1960−61	1969−70	1960−61	1969−70
Church	4.9%	2.2%	5.5%	1.7%	39.0%	40.2%
Students (tuition and other payments)	75.4%	79.6%	77.6%	66.4%	2.8%	11.7%
Endowments	8.9%	4.9%	12.6%	6.3%	11.1%	11.7%
Other	10.8%	13.3%	4.3%	25.6%	47.1%	35.7%

NOTE: Due to insufficient data, Tougaloo College and Butler University are not included in these statistics.

Sources of additional income. The data in table 14 suggest that the related colleges have sought additional income principally by increasing tuition and student enrollment in addition to increasing contributions from alumni, foundations, and other donors. The universities have sought additional income principally from alumni, foundations, and other sources. The schools of religion have increased income principally from students, presumably through some partial tuition payment via their related universities.

Role of Disciples-related colleges and universities in the development of professional ministers. To indicate the significant role that these related institutions play in the process of ministerial formation in the Christian Church, table 15 provides a yearly analysis of the undergraduate origins of Disciples seminarians from 1961 to 1971.

From 1961 to 1971, the number of Disciples seminarians decreased by

TABLE 15
UNDERGRADUATE ORIGINS OF SEMINARY STUDENTS
(Disciples Students—Fall Semester)

	Disciples-related	% Disciples	Public	% Disciples	Private	% Disciples	Others	% Disciples	Special and Unknown	% Disciples	GRAND TOTAL
1961−62	458	60	116	15	104	14	45	6	46	6	769
1962−63	448	60	119	16	88	12	44	6	52	7	751
1963−64	431	61	122	17	83	17	39	6	32	5	707
1964−65	409	58	133	19	82	12	43	6	37	5	704
1965−66	400	56	137	19	84	12	51	7	40	6	712
1966−67	353	54	128	20	83	13	50	8	35	5	649
1967−68	344	53	157	24	64	10	58	9	20	3	643
1968−69	345	58	134	23	51	9	41	7	22	4	593
1969−70	338	55	149	24	66	11	49	8	14	2	616
1970−71	323	53	153	25	65	11	45	7	23	4	609
1971−72	318	54	152	26	56	10	43	7	15	3	584
Total	4,167	57	1,500	20	826	11	508	7	336	5	7,337

NOTE: 1961−71 Trends:

30.6% decrease of number of Disciples seminary students from Disciples undergraduate institutions—a 6% decrease in proportion—trend downward.

53.8% decrease of number of Disciples seminary students from private undergraduate institutions—a 4% decrease in proportion—trend downward.

24.1% decrease of Disciples seminary students—trend leveling out around 600 students.

32.2% increase of number of seminary students from public undergraduate institutions—an 11% increase in proportion—trend upward.

Number of Disciples seminary students from other church-related colleges remaining constant.

24.1%, leveling off at about six hundred each year for the last four years. There was a 30.6% decrease of seminarians graduated from Disciples-related undergraduate institutions, a 53.8% decrease of seminarians graduated from private undergraduate institutions, and a 32.2% increase of seminarians graduated from state undergraduate institutions. The number of seminarians graduated from other church-related undergraduate institutions remained about the same.

In the fall of 1971, about 66% of the nation's undergraduate and graduate students were enrolled in public institutions. In contrast, about 75% of enrolled Disciples seminarians had graduated from some type of private undergraduate institution, 54% from Disciples-related institutions.[4]

Table 16 shows the undergraduate origins, by institution, of Disciples seminarians, 1961 to 1971, who graduated from Disciples-related colleges and universities. These data show that the 30.6% decrease of Disciples seminarians coming from Disciples-related undergraduate institutions was a fairly evenly distributed decline among all these institutions, most of

4. The number of seminarians graduated from public institutions who were enrolled in related schools of religion is unknown.

TABLE 16
UNDERGRADUATE ORIGINS OF SEMINARY STUDENTS
(Disciples Students—Fall Semester)

	ACC	% Disciples	Bethany	% Disciples	Butler	% Disciples	Chapman	% Disciples	Culver	% Disciples	Drake	% Disciples	Eureka	% Disciples	Hiram	% Disciples	Jarvis	% Disciples	Lynchburg	% Disciples	NCC	% Disciples	Phillips	% Disciples	TCU	% Disciples	Transylvania	% Disciples	TOTALS
1961–62	20	4	24	5	27	6	13	3	21	5	15	3	14	3	9	2	4	1	24	5	81	18	101	22	73	16	32	7	458
1962–63	15	4	30	7	27	6	15	3	17	4	17	4	13	5	9	2	5	1	27	6	65	15	104	23	67	15	27	6	448
1963–64	17	4	30	7	15	3	12	3	15	3	14	3	14	3	12	3	4	1	25	6	90	21	86	20	67	16	30	7	431
1964–65	17	4	21	5	20	5	13	3	15	4	14	2	14	3	15	4	4	1	19	5	90	22	83	20	62	15	27	6	409
1965–66	19	5	22	6	11	3	16	4	16	4	16	4	17	4	12	4	4	1	19	5	84	21	71	18	66	17	24	6	400
1966–67	17	5	19	5	15	4	15	4	17	5	9	3	14	4	9	3	0	0	15	4	85	24	61	17	54	15	20	6	353
1967–68	17	5	24	5	8	2	14	4	15	4	10	3	11	3	5	1	0	0	13	4	83	24	69	20	53	15	18	5	344
1968–69	16	5	22	6	7	2	14	4	17	5	9	3	11	3	6	2	2	1	16	5	74	21	67	19	66	20	21	6	345
1969–70	13	4	23	7	6	2	16	5	24	7	10	3	10	3	11	3	2	1	16	5	68	20	60	18	64	19	20	6	338
1970–71	14	4	19	6	4	1	15	5	33	10	8	3	9	3	10	3	3	1	11	3	58	18	59	18	62	19	19	6	323
1971–72	10	3	19	6	2	1	15	5	31	10	4	1	3	1	10	2	2	1	16	5	59	10	61	19	54	17	28	9	318

NOTE: Related colleges having very few graduates in seminary are not included.

NOTE: 1961–71 trends:
There was a generally distributed decline of seminary enrollment from Disciples-related colleges and universities. The proportion of decline was fairly evenly distributed; Butler University was a significant exception. Culver-Stockton College had the only significant increase.

them producing about the same proportion of seminary students, 1961 compared to 1971. Butler University and Culver-Stockton College are exceptions; Butler University had a significant decline, Culver-Stockton College a significant increase.

It is interesting that these same institutions differ markedly in financial support received from the Christian Church. Butler University did not receive any financial support from the church during the 1960s. During the same period, church contributions to Culver-Stockton for operating expenses increased 220%.

Primary source of seminarians. *From 1961 to 1971, three institutions produced over 50% of all Disciples seminarians graduating from Disciples-related colleges and universities.* Northwest Christian College had an average of 76.1 Disciples students enrolled each year in seminary. Phillips University had an average of 74.7 graduates enrolled in seminary, and Texas Christian University had an average of 62.5 graduates enrolled. Respectively, these averages are 20.1%, 19.7%, and 16.5% of the annual average of 378.9 Disciples seminarians graduated from Disciples-related institutions. Combined, they total 56.3% of this group and 32% of the annual average of all Disciples seminarians.

Correlation of church support and numbers of seminarians. *In 1970-71, these same three institutions received the three largest amounts of financial support from the Christian Church,* comprising 35.9% of all that was given to the eighteen related colleges and universities. Further analysis shows that there is a very high correlation between church contributions to the eighteen related institutions and their annual average of graduates enrolled in seminary over the past eleven years.[5] That is, those institutions which produce more professional leaders for the church receive more financial support from the church; those which produce fewer professional leaders receive less.

Correlation does not prove causation. It does suggest, however, *that the procedures by which the church allocates its financial support to related colleges and universities are responsive to a principal concern of the church, professional leadership development.* These data also suggest that *where the church maintains relatedness and support of its colleges and universities, these educational institutions seek to serve the church in return.*

B. UNDERGRADUATE PROGRAMS OF MINISTERIAL EDUCATION

Role of undergraduate and graduate educational programs. Bridston and Culver in their study of preseminary education identify four major components in the educational development of effective

5. Spearman's rank-difference correlation method computed a .6987, statistically significant at the .01 confidence level with an N of 18.

ministers—religious faith, liberal-cultural education, professional competence, and vocational integration. They further suggest that the primary domains of undergraduate ministerial education are spiritual and liberal-cultural education, while the primary domains of graduate seminary education are continued spiritual development, professional competence, and vocational integration.[6]

Myron T. Hopper suggested a similar division of labor for ministerial education at a 1953 conference on education for Disciples ministers at Lexington Theological Seminary (then College of the Bible):

In general, it can be said that the college should offer the broad general education which should provide for reasonable competency in all fields of knowledge, orientation in the culture, and an understanding of people and how they grow and develop. There should be, of course, such orientation in religion as should be possessed by all educated people and there should, also, be those experiences needed to nurture the religious growth of the undergraduate student. The seminary, on the other hand, should emphasize professional training which would include intensive study in the area of religion and the development of the skills and understandings especially needed by religious leaders.[7]

General pattern of education. The general pattern of undergraduate ministerial education provided by the majority of the related colleges, universities, and schools of religion can be described as liberal arts education supplemented by varying types of spiritual and professional nurture, guidance, and experience. The program at Northwest Christian College is an exception, offering instruction in the practice of ministerial functions.

Cultivation of religious faith. Unlike ministerial students of other denominations, over 50% of Disciples ministerial students major in religion at the undergraduate level. Most of the related institutions provide chapels, prayer groups, Bible study groups, and other small-group experiences for cultivation of religious faith. In some cases, e.g., Texas Christian University, Phillips University, Atlantic Christian College, Culver-Stockton College, and Northwest Christian College, upper-division students assume field work assignments in nearby congregations. Most of this field work is not supervised or well integrated into the formal educational program.

Staffing for ministerial education. In some cases, e.g., Culver-

6. Keith R. Bridston and Dwight W. Culver, *Pre-seminary Education* (Minneapolis: Augsburg Publishing House, 1965).

7. HowardElmo Short, ed., *Education for the Christian Ministry for Tomorrow's Church* (Lexington: College of the Bible, 1953), pp. 39—40. Used by permission of Lexington Theological Seminary.

Stockton College and Atlantic Christian College, a member of the faculty or staff is assigned responsibility for guiding, advising, recruiting, and supervising ministerial students. Generally, however, that responsibility is shared by professors of religion, college chaplains, directors of church relations, etc. Those institutions which have clearly delegated primary responsibility for ministerial education to one of their staff appear to have more effective programs.

A series of interviews at Culver-Stockton College led to the conclusion that the unusual increase in ministerial productivity in that institution is due to a confluence of forces:

1. Sincere and intense interest in the professional ministry of the church by major administrators and professors
2. Close coordination and rapport between the college and all manifestations of the Christian Church
3. Provision of personnel and budget to coordinate effectively the various aspects of ministerial development

Education for lay leadership. Some institutions, e.g., Atlantic Christian College, Culver-Stockton College, Eureka College, Christian College of Georgia, Northwest Christian College, and the Missouri School of Religion, offer courses, on and off campus, for lay theological education and leadership development. Some of these courses have been jointly sponsored with the Department of Ministry and Worship. As the Christian Church experiences increasing needs for lay preachers, bivocational ministers, etc., it is likely that institutions of this type will be sought out for increased efforts in this style of ministerial education.

Summary observations. The following is a summary of the commission's observations regarding undergraduate education for ministry based on the above data and other information:

1. *Related undergraduate colleges and universities play an essential role in the development of the professional ministry of the church.* It appears that the schools of religion do not make a significant contribution to ministerial education. However, more research is needed to investigate this observation.
2. The primary functions of related colleges and universities in ministerial development are:
   a. Interpretation, recruitment, and guidance for the profession of ministry[8]

---

8. For conclusions of the report on the National Cooperative Enlistment Project, which suggest the most effective means of ministerial interpretation and recruitment at the undergraduate level, see Lewis G. Douglass, *The Church Reaching Out: Interpreting Ministry as a Career* (New York: IDOC, 1970), pp. 78–80.

    b. The development of liberally educated ministerial students who are able to assume graduate level, professional study upon graduation

    c. The development of the religious faith and spiritual life of ministerial students

    d. Sufficient exposure to the practice of ministry to maintain realistic appraisal of the function of ministry in the institutional church and other institutional structures

    e. Provision of educational experiences for special types of ministers—lay preachers, bivocational ministers, lay leaders, etc.

    f. In some cases, continuing education for ministers, particularly in liberal arts, business, etc.

3. Each of the twenty-three related educational institutions is independent, governed by a Board of Trustees which is self-perpetuating. These institutions remain related to the Christian Church by free choice, symbolized and actualized by membership in the Board of Higher Education of the church. Bonds of relatedness with the church are many and varied. Some of these are:

    a. Historical and traditional bonds

    b. Mutual purposes, e.g., search for truth, development of persons, provision of a forum for the interaction of faith and learning

    c. Mutual goals, e.g., leadership development for the church and society

    d. Programs of mutual assistance and support

    Given the current situation in higher education and the Christian Church, there are many forces that threaten relatedness between these institutions and the church. Chief among these are the increasing financial stress that the institutions are undergoing and the relative decline of financial support and student enrollment provided by the Christian Church. As these educational institutions become more dependent on sources of financial support outside the church, there will be less reason and perhaps less opportunity for them to serve the interests and needs of the church.

4. At present, effective programs of ministerial development at these related institutions seem to be the result of sincere interest in the church and its leadership on the part of major administrators and faculty. In some cases, change of leadership of these institutions has radically altered the quality and degree of relatedness with the church. It would seem that structured lines of communication and

relationship between institutions and church at the point of the church's principal needs might ensure a more lasting and secure relatedness. This principle has implications for changes in staffing patterns and policy influence on programs of undergraduate ministerial education. These implications will be explored in the concluding section on recommendations.

C. RELATED GRADUATE THEOLOGICAL INSTITUTIONS

Historical sketch. Completion of a seminary program of study is normative for those who seek the office of ordained minister in the order of ministry of the Christian Church.[9] A profile of 1,988 ordained ministers who were members of the Pension Fund in 1968 found that 77% had completed a seminary program. This percentage is high compared with that for most other American Protestant denominations. It is remarkable when one considers that the Disciples established their first graduate seminary less than thirty-five years ago. In 1938 the College of the Bible in Lexington, Kentucky, was established as a wholly graduate seminary. Until that date, most Disciples who pursued graduate theological education did so at other denominational or university seminaries. Some enrolled at the University of Chicago Divinity School through the Disciples Divinity House, which was founded in 1894.

Riley B. Montgomery, in the most complete study of Disciples ministerial education on record, found that in 1926 only 17.2% of Disciples ministers had both college and seminary training. He further found that the Disciples of Christ, compared with twenty other denominations, ranked in the middle relative to the educational level of their ministry.[10]

In little more than thirty years, the percentage of the clergy of the Christian Church having completed graduate seminary training increased from one-fifth to four-fifths.

This was accomplished primarily by the institutions of graduate theological education related to the Christian Church. The following information describes each of these institutions in considerable detail:

Related institutions. In 1961 the Christian Church listed six seminaries and four foundation houses as related to the church through the Board of Higher Education.

---

9. "Policies and Criteria for the Order of Ministry in the Christian Church (Disciples of Christ)," Section II, C.

10. Riley B. Montgomery, *The Education of Ministers of Disciples of Christ* (St. Louis: Bethany Press, 1931), p. 103.

The six *seminaries* comprise three distinguishable types of institutions:

1. Seminaries within a private, church-related university: Brite Divinity School of Texas Christian University in Fort Worth, Texas; Drake Divinity School of Drake University in Des Moines, Iowa; and the Graduate Seminary of Phillips University in Enid, Oklahoma.
2. A seminary affiliated with a program of instruction in religion at a state university campus: Missouri School of Religion in Columbia, Missouri.
3. Seminaries not organically related to universities: Christian Theological Seminary, Indianapolis, Indiana, and Lexington Theological Seminary, Lexington, Kentucky. Historically, these institutions were related, respectively, to Butler University and Transylvania University.

The four *foundation houses* are resident academic communities established and supported by the denomination in relation to non-Disciples seminaries. Basically, they are subcommunities of these seminaries, making use of and contributing to the instructional process there. The houses can be characterized as two types:

1. Those related to divinity schools of major private universities: Disciples Divinity House at the University of Chicago in Chicago, Illinois; Disciples Divinity House at Vanderbilt University in Nashville, Tennessee; and New Haven Disciples House at Yale University, New Haven, Connecticut.
2. A house related to a denominational seminary: Disciples Seminary Foundation of the School of Theology at Claremont, California, a United Methodist seminary.

By fall, 1972, only four seminaries and three foundation houses were related through the Board of Higher Education. (See table 17 for a capsule description of these institutions.) Drake Divinity School closed its program at the end of the 1967–68 year. Missouri School of Religion, the only unaccredited Disciples seminary, decided to phase out its seminary program at the end of the 1971–72 academic year in order to use its full resources in the undergraduate program of instruction in religion. Disciples House at Yale Divinity School changed its program to the Ecumenical Continuing Education Center and withdrew from the Board of Higher Education in the fall of 1968.

In addition to the above institutions, Disciples students have continued to enroll in numerous seminaries throughout the United States and Canada. The largest collection of these students is normally found at Yale

TABLE 17
DESCRIPTION OF GRADUATE THEOLOGICAL
INSTITUTIONS RELATED TO THE CHRISTIAN CHURCH (DISCIPLES OF CHRIST)

Name and Location of Institutions	Founding Date as Graduate Seminary	Parent Institution	Degrees Granted	Enrollment		1970–71 Operating Expenses (in Thousands of Dollars)
				Total—Fall, 1972	Disciples	
Seminaries Within Universities						
Brite Divinity School Fort Worth, Texas	1939	Texas Christian University	Master of Divinity Master of Religious Education Master of Theology Doctor of Ministry	202	112	$ 493
Phillips Graduate Seminary Enid, Oklahoma	1940[1]	Phillips University	Master of Divinity Master of Religious Education Doctor of Ministry	121	70	263
Independent Seminaries						
Christian Theological Seminary Indianapolis, Indiana	1958		Master of Arts in Religion Master of Divinity Master of Ministry Doctor of Ministry	262	90	1,329
Lexington Theological Seminary Lexington, Kentucky	1936		Master of Divinity Master of Religious Education Doctor of Ministry	110	83	641
Foundation Houses						
Disciples Divinity House Chicago, Illinois	1894	University of Chicago Divinity School	Master of Arts Doctor of Ministry Doctor of Philosophy		18	110
Disciples Divinity House Nashville, Tennessee	1927	Vanderbilt University The Divinity School	Master of Divinity Doctor of Ministry		50	41
Disciples Seminary Foundation Claremont, California	1960	Claremont School of Theology	Master of Religion Doctor of Ministry Doctor of Philosophy Doctor of Theology		32	83

[1] Previous graduate/professional work was provided at the master's level.

Divinity School, Union Theological Seminary in New York City, and Pacific School of Religion in Berkeley, California, the latter having a formal relationship to the regional church in northern California and Nevada.

Enrollments. An analysis of the enrollments in Disciples seminaries and Disciples students in both Disciples and non-Disciples theological schools for the years 1961 to 1972 is provided in tables 18 and 19.

TABLE 18
ENROLLMENT IN DISCIPLES SEMINARIES

Academic Year	Brite Divinity School	Christian Theological Seminary	Drake Divinity School	Phillips Graduate Seminary	Lexington Theological Seminary	Missouri School of Religion	Total
1961−62	168	236	62	118	128	32	744
	(138)	(144)	(38)	(98)	(119)	(25)	(562)
	82%	61%	61%	83%	93%	78%	76%
1962−63	172	236	63	92	132	42	737
	(134)	(136)	(34)	(80)	(116)	(32)	(532)
	78%	58%	54%	87%	88%	76%	72%
1963−64	178	209	58	92	126	31	694
	(133)	(123)	(28)	(77)	(112)	(23)	(496)
	75%	59%	48%	84%	89%	74%	71%
1964−65	156	214	60	106	130	35	701
	(120)	(119)	(32)	(88)	(103)	(27)	(489)
	77%	56%	53%	83%	79%	77%	70%
1965−66	150	215	67	93	119	32	676
	(111)	(121)	(41)	(74)	(100)	(21)	(468)
	74%	56%	61%	80%	84%	66%	69%
1966−67	122	255	69	100	108	24	678
	(91)	(127)	(34)	(82)	(91)	(19)	(444)
	75%	50%	49%	82%	84%	79%	65%
1967−68	141	255	55	107	102	23	683
	(86)	(117)	(26)	(88)	(95)	(16)	(428)
	61%	46%	47%	82%	93%	70%	63%
1968−69	148	229	closed	112	94	20	603
	(87)	(102)		(85)	(75)	(13)	(362)
	59%	44%		76%	80%	65%	60%
1969−70	158	256		102	98	23	637
	(101)	(113)		(73)	(79)	(13)	(379)
	64%	44%		72%	81%	57%	59%
1970−71	195	300		109	109	22	735
	(120)	(112)		(62)	(68)	(16)	(378)
	62%	37%		57%	62%	73%	51%
1971−72	211	268		123	112	22	736
	(118)	(99)		(72)	(82)	(14)	(385)
	56%	37%		59%	73%	64%	52%
1972−73	202	262		121	110	closed	695
	(112)	(90)		(70)	(83)		(355)
	55%	34%		58%	75%		51%

NOTE: Top number in each group = total enrollment, all categories, fall of each year, AATS reports; number in parentheses = total Disciples enrollment, fall of each year, based on BHE reports; % = ratio of Disciples enrollment to total enrollment.

TABLE 19

TOTAL ENROLLMENT OF DISCIPLES SEMINARY STUDENTS

Academic Year	Disciples Seminaries	Foundation Houses			Non-Disciples Seminaries	Total[1]
		DDH-C[2]	DDH-V[3]	DSF[4]		
1961−62	562	33	42	7	84	769
1962−63	532	32	45	14	83	751
1963−64	496	29	50	23	72	707
1964−65	489	27	47	29	78	704
1965−66	468	26	58	30	89	712
1966−67	444	17	50	34	78	649
1967−68	428	14	57	39	86	643
1968−69	362	18	62	38	90	593
1969−70	379	16	60	47	114	616
1970−71	378	19	60	41	111	609
1971−72	385	9	59	40	91	584
1972−73	355	18	50	32	89	544

[1] Includes all categories of students for the fall semester of each year based on Board of Higher Education reports.

[2] Disciples Divinity House, University of Chicago.

[3] Disciples Divinity House, Vanderbilt University.

[4] Disciples Seminary Foundation, School of Theology at Claremont.

Seminary enrollment trends. The total fall enrollment of Disciples seminaries experienced periodic declines from 744 students in 1961 to 600 students in 1968. In 1969 and 1970, sizable enrollment increases occurred; 637 and 735 students were enrolled, respectively. In the fall of 1971, 736 students were enrolled; 695 in fall, 1972. In 1969−70 and 1970−71, Disciples seminaries had the largest percentage (16.5%) of increase in enrollment among denominational seminaries holding membership in the American Association of Theological Schools. This increase was due principally to the enrollment of students pursuing the newly instituted Doctor of Ministry degree.[11]

In 1961, 76% of the students enrolled in Disciples seminaries were Disciples (range: 61% to 93% among the seminaries). In 1972, 51% of the students were Disciples (range: 34% to 75%). In 1961, 182 non-Disciples were enrolled in Disciples seminaries and 84 Disciples were enrolled in non-Disciples seminaries, a ratio of 2.2 to 1, respectively. In 1972, 340 non-Disciples were enrolled in Disciples seminaries and 89 Disciples were enrolled in non-Disciples seminaries, a ratio of 3.8 to 1. (Foundation houses are not included in this statistic.)

Decreasing enrollment of Disciples students. The total enrollment of Disciples seminary students, all Disciples in all seminaries throughout the United States and Canada, decreased 29.3%, from 769 students in 1961 to 544 students in 1972; a 36.8% decrease in Disciples seminaries, an

11. *A.A.T.S. Fact Book on Theological Education 1971−72*, p. 8.

18.7% decrease in foundation houses, and an increase of 6.0% in the non-Disciples seminaries. The trend of this decrease was periodic decline through 1968. The total number of Disciples enrolled stayed around 600 per year from 1969 to 1971. In the fall of 1972, total enrollment declined to 544.

Analysis of the undergraduate origins of Disciples seminarians was given in the section on undergraduate ministerial education (pp. 51-53).

Enrollment in first professional degree program. There has been a general downward trend (39% from 1961 to 1971) of students enrolled in the first professional degree program in seminaries. However, there is a marked increase in the enrollment of Disciples in advanced degree programs in seminaries. The bulk of this increase (65% from 1961 to 1971) occurred in 1970 and 1971 and is due primarily to enrollment for the Doctor of Ministry degree.

Women seminarians. In 1970 sixty-two women (8.4% of all students) were enrolled in Disciples seminaries. Twenty-eight of these women were Disciples and comprised 5.6% of all Disciples enrolled in seminaries.

Minority students. In 1971 six black Disciples and one Hispanic-American Disciple, or 1.1% minority students, were enrolled in seminaries in the United States and Canada.

Attrition and graduation. A larger proportion of Disciples seminarians from Disciples undergraduate institutions received degrees (57% of enrollment/67.5% of degrees) than Disciples seminarians from publicly supported or other private institutions (43% of enrollment/36.6% of degrees).

Practice of ministry. About two-thirds of Disciples students who enrolled during the 1960s as first-year seminarians are listed in the *1970–1971 Year Book* as practicing some form of professional ministry for the Christian Church.

D. GRADUATE THEOLOGICAL EDUCATION PROGRAMS

Types of programs. The seven institutions of graduate theological education related to the Christian Church provide a rich diversity of educational programs. They are designed to meet the diverse educational needs of the church and varied interests of students. Basically, there are four types of programs:

1. Professional ministerial programs preparing students for ordination.
2. Professional programs in specialized ministries that may or may not prepare students for ordination. These may be taken by lay persons, students pursuing ordination, or ordained ministers who seek to develop specialized ministries.

3. Continuing education programs for professional ministers who seek to maintain and/or advance their expertise in ministry.
4. Academic studies in religion not designed to prepare students for ordination but to teach students modes of inquiry into the academic discipline of religion and acquaint them with significant literature in the field. Some students use these programs, normally at the doctoral level, to prepare for teaching at the college, university, or seminary level and subsequently seek ordination for a specialized ministry of the church. Other students may take these programs to pursue an educational interest or to prepare for teaching, but may not seek ordination.

Degrees. The degrees that relate to these programs have changed greatly in recent years. Presently, eight different degrees are offered among the seven institutions. All institutions offer professional degrees that relate to program types 1 and 2 above. These are distinguished as first professional and advanced professional degrees. The course of study for these degrees varies from two to four years of full-time study. In some cases the same degree (Doctor of Ministry) is viewed by one institution as a first professional degree, by others as an advanced professional degree.

Master of Divinity degree. The majority of these institutions offer the Master of Divinity as the basic first professional degree for the ordained ministry. It has replaced the former Bachelor of Divinity degree. It is usually three years of full-time study requiring (1) coursework in the broad areas of Bible, church history, theology, church administration, and pastoral care; and (2) field education in some functional context of ministry, normally a congregational type. Through two of the foundation houses, the four-year Doctor of Ministry is offered as the first professional degree.

Master of Religious Education and Master of Ministry degrees. Four of the institutions offer first professional degree programs for specialized ministries such as Christian education, church music, pastoral care and counseling, communication, and community ministries. The degrees are Master of Religious Education and Master of Ministry. The course of study is two years of full-time work: normally one year of general theological studies and one year of specialized studies including field education.

Master of Theology and Doctor of Ministry degrees. Five of the institutions, which do not offer the Doctor of Ministry as a first professional degree, offer the Master of Theology and/or the Doctor of Ministry degree for advanced professional education. The course of study is an additional one to one and one-half years of full-time work beyond the Master of

Divinity or Bachelor of Divinity degree. Generally, instruction is more specialized and individualized, using seminars rather than lectures, focusing more on the development of excellence in professional skills, involving more intensely supervised field education, and requiring high-level research on functional problems of ministry.

Degrees at foundation houses. All three foundation houses and two of the seminaries provide academic studies in religion. All offer a master's degree for the first two years of study. In addition, the three seminaries with whom the foundation houses relate offer doctoral degrees in their advanced academic programs. These are generally modeled after traditional university Ph.D.'s with heavy emphasis on research in highly specialized subject areas.

Nondegree programs. In addition to these degree programs, each of these institutions offers a wide variety of noncredit courses, seminars, and other short-term events for the education of laity and the continuing education of professional ministers.

Decade of degrees. From 1961−62 to 1970−71, 1,360 degrees from graduate theological institutions related to the Board of Higher Education were awarded to Disciples students. Of these, 1,239, or 91.1%, were first professional degrees; 84, or 6.2%, were advanced professional degrees; and 37, or 2.7%, were academic degrees.[12] An additional 114 first professional degrees and 1 advanced professional degree were awarded to Disciples by theological institutions not related to the Board of Higher Education.[13]

Predominance of professional degrees. These statistics show that *the vast majority (91.7%) of theological degrees conferred on Disciples seminarians in the past ten years were first professional degrees, designed to prepare students for one of the ministries of the church. Institutions related to the Board of Higher Education awarded 91.6% of these first professional degrees.*

Obviously, Disciples-related seminaries and foundation houses continue to train the vast majority of the professional ministry of the Christian Church. In addition, they are providing training for an increasing number of professional ministers of other denominations.

From graduation to ministry. Other research indicates that the vast majority of Disciples who receive first professional degrees from related seminaries assume a ministerial post within the Christian Church. For example, 86.9% (245 of 282) of the Disciples who received first professional degrees from Disciples seminaries and foundation houses in 1967 and 1968 had ministerial standing in 1971. One hundred seventy-eight (72.7%) of

12. Degrees awarded by Butler University not included.
13. Early records are not complete.

these were full-time ministers in congregations, seventeen (6.9%) were students or bivocational ministers, and the remaining 20.4% were in a variety of full-time specialized ministries.

Faculties. The four accredited seminaries of the Christian Church in the year 1971–72 had a combined faculty of fifty-seven full-time and thirteen part-time members, or a full-time equivalent faculty of sixty-one and one-third persons. Dividing the 736 students enrolled in 1971 by this full-time equivalent figure gives a faculty-student ratio of one to twelve.

All seventy faculty members are men. Sixty-nine are white, one is black. The average age of the faculty is about forty-eight years, with a range of thirty to sixty-five years. Forty-four (63%) of these have an earned doctor's degree, sixty (86%) have had some experience in the pastoral ministry, and fifty-one (73%) are Disciples. Among the four accredited seminaries, the average nine-month salary of the full-time faculty ranges from about $11,300 to $14,300, excluding fringe benefits.

Libraries. The four accredited seminaries have library collections ranging in size from 50,000 to 130,000 volumes. These holdings are supplemented by a variety of interinstitutional consortia that permit students to use the resources of other libraries.

The library resources available to students in the foundation houses have collections for the study of ministry and religion ranging from 105,-000 to 160,000 volumes. These holdings are supplemented by much larger university holdings in a variety of fields.

Diverse patterns of finance. The financial picture of these institutions of theological education is very complex and diverse, making it most difficult to provide useful comparisons. For example, the three foundation houses differ widely from one another. The Disciples Divinity House at Chicago has a sizable endowment that supplies 78% of its revenue for operating expenses. Disciples Divinity House at Vanderbilt receives generous scholarship support from university funds (unlike the other two houses) and is thereby able to support many students on limited funds. In addition, the dean receives half of his salary from Vanderbilt University for teaching responsibilities. Disciples Seminary Foundation at Claremont not only funds all scholarship aid given to Disciples students, but provides partial financial support for a professorship in the seminary in addition to the full salary of the director.

Brite Divinity School and Phillips Graduate Seminary are seminaries within universities. Some of the costs of their programs are included within university expenses with little or no charge made to the seminaries. For example, Texas Christian University provides Brite with a library facility, maintenance of its buildings, some purchases of equipment, business office services, and other administrative services at no charge to the Brite program. In addition, students enrolled at Brite and Phillips seminaries receive sizable tuition discounts.

Christian Theological Seminary and Lexington Theological Seminary provide the most complete picture of the total cost of seminary education. However, the style of theological education that each is pursuing varies greatly. Therefore, a simple comparison of financial statistics fails to deal adequately with their differences.

In conclusion, contrary to much current thought, there is at present no way to use available financial statistics to make meaningful comparisons of economic efficiency among institutions. The primary value of financial statistics is to examine the picture of each institution as a separate unit or all institutions as a combined system, rather than on a comparative basis.

With all the above complexities, selected statistics are presented, reporting the combined financial picture of the institutions of graduate theological education, based on the 1970−71 fiscal year.

Average cost per student. The average operating cost per student figure among all seven accredited institutions for 1970−71 was $3,008 ($3,247 among the seminaries and $1,588 among the foundation houses). These figures do not include capital expenses or student aid expenses. The average operating cost per degree awarded was $16,929 ($18,229) among the seminaries and $9,072 among the foundation houses). The range of cost per student among all eight institutions was $242 to $5,584. The range of cost per degree awarded among all eight institutions was $2,824 to $25,362.

Church contributions per Disciples student. In 1970−71 the average operating contribution per Disciples student from the Christian Church among all accredited graduate theological institutions was $1,368 ($1,615 among the seminaries and $621 among the foundation houses). The operating contribution per Disciples degree recipient was $7,249 ($8,-354 among the seminaries and $3,551 among the foundation houses). Church contributions met 45.5% of the cost-per-student figure and 42.8% of the cost-per-degree figure.

Cost comparison with other denominations. Chart 1 reports the cost-per-student figure among eighty-nine seminaries grouped by their denominational affiliation. Among eleven denominations, the $3,118 cost-per-student figure for five Disciples-related seminaries (Missouri School of Religion included) for 1970−71 ranks ninth (range: $5,681 to $1,601; average for all seminaries: $2,929). These data indicate that, *in relationship to other denominations, seminaries related to the Christian Church are financially efficient.* If these statistics included similar data

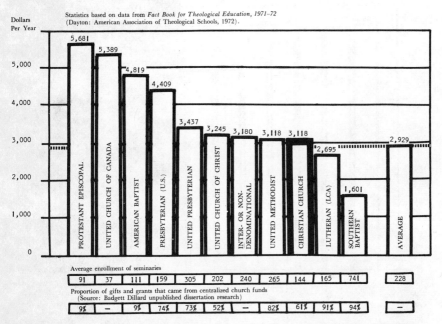

CHART 1

OPERATING COST PER STUDENT AMONG SEMINARIES
COMPARISON BY DENOMINATIONAL AFFILIATION

(1970–71)

from the foundation houses and deleted Missouri School of Religion figures, the cost-per-student figure would be even more favorable comparatively.

Correlation of size and cost. As the enrollment figures at the bottom of chart 1 show, there is a definite relationship between the average size of the seminaries of each denomination and their average cost per student. (Correlation of .6708, significant at the .05 level of confidence, computed by the Spearman rank-difference method.) However, the relatively high cost per student of Presbyterian (U.S.) seminaries and the relatively low cost per student of Lutheran (L.C.A.) and Disciples seminaries suggest that factors other than size are important influences on economic efficiency.

Charts 2 and 3 suggest that Disciples seminaries maintain a relatively low cost-per-student figure while operating relatively smaller seminaries by paying relatively low faculty and administrative salaries. For example, among eleven denominations, Disciples seminaries rank ninth in average cost per student, ninth in average faculty compensation, and ninth in average administrative compensation.

CHART 2

AVERAGE FACULTY COMPENSATION
COMPARISON BY DENOMINATIONAL AFFILIATION

(1971–72)

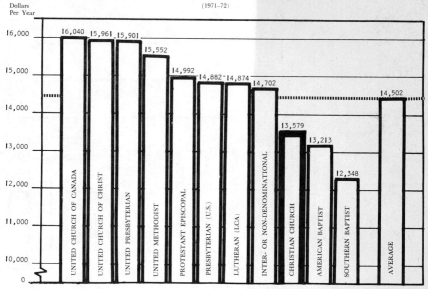

Dollars
Per Year

CHART 3

AVERAGE ADMINISTRATION COMPENSATION
COMPARISON BY DENOMINATIONAL AFFILIATION

(1971–72)

Dollars
Per Year

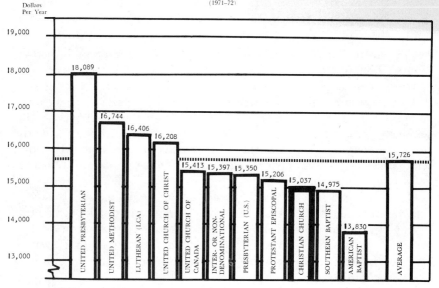

However, relatively low faculty and administrative compensation have not prevented American Baptist seminaries from having a relatively high cost-per-student figure. Similarly, the Lutheran (L.C.A.) seminaries seem to be relatively small, provide better than average faculty and administrative salaries, and still maintain a relatively low cost-per-student rank.

Cost and financial support patterns. The line of percentages at the bottom of chart 1 indicates the ratio of gift and grant support that comes from national and regional church sources as compared to direct support from local congregations, groups within congregations, church foundations, individuals, and other sources. Using these percentages as measures of centralized church financial support, a correlation of .825 with the cost-per-student figure was computed, significant at the .01 level, using the Spearman rank-difference method.

Combined with the above findings, this seems to suggest that *those denominations which have centralized their financial support of seminaries have been able to effect relative economic efficiency among them.* In some cases, for example, Southern Baptist seminaries, this has been accomplished through larger seminaries and lower average salaries for faculty and administration. In other cases, for example, Lutheran (L.C.A.) seminaries, how economies are effected is not revealed by these data.

Financial efficiency. These data and other impressions lead to the general observation that *financial efficiency of seminaries is highly affected by such factors as (1) regional location, (2) organizational style and relationships, (3) socioeconomic milieu of the supporting denomination, (4) patterns of control and accountability between institutional parent and institutional offspring (e.g., seminary-denomination, seminary-university, foundation house-seminary).* Indeed, these may be more formative of the finances of an institution than the single factor of size alone.

Denominational comparisons of costs. An analysis of the sources of operating income among our eight institutions of graduate education reveals considerable diversity of sources. Table 20 presents these data.

Increasing tuition costs. From 1961 to 1971, tuition charges among Disciples institutions of graduate theological education rose from an average of $461 per year to $1,252 per year, or 272%. Among seminaries the average charge rose from $394 per year to $868 per year, or 220%. Among foundation houses the average charge rose from $573 per year to $1,892 per year, or 330%.

Costs to students. The estimated costs for a married couple with no children, including educational and living expenses, 1971−72, vary from

$4,500 to $8,000. The seminaries generally estimate a lower cost than the foundation houses. However, every institution offers considerable financial aid to reduce the actual expense to the student. In some instances, tuition, fees, and room and board costs are covered through financial aid. In most cases, students do not pay the full tuition charge from their own resources.

TABLE 20
RELATED GRADUATE THEOLOGICAL INSTITUTIONS:
SOURCES OF OPERATING INCOME

Source of Operating Income	Range of Proportion of Income Among Institutions	Average Proportion of Income Among Institutions
Church	8% to 62%	22.4%
Tuition and fees	10% to 46%	15.6%
Endowment	2% to 78%	28.4%
Gifts	6% to 40%	14.4%
Other	4% to 31%	19.2%

Increasing deficits. In 1970–71 the five seminaries experienced a total operating deficit of $235,517; this was an average deficit of $42,103 per seminary, or $320.43 per student. The foundation houses experienced a $9,640 operating surplus; this was an average surplus of $3,213 per house, or $803.33 per student. All five seminaries had an operating deficit for 1970–71. The deficits of Phillips Graduate Seminary and Brite Divinity School were absorbed by their related universities. Christian Theological Seminary, Lexington Theological Seminary, and Missouri School of Religion covered their deficits by use of reserve funds or loans secured against endowment and plant. These latter three institutions experienced increasing accumulative deficits in the 1960s and early 1970s. This factor was highly influential in the decision to phase out the graduate seminary program of the Missouri School of Religion. Lexington Theological Seminary is currently budgeting $100,000 of its annual operating budget for debt retirement. Christian Theological Seminary is budgeting $10,000 of its operating budget for debt retirement.

Table 21 indicates changes among related seminaries and foundations in operating expenses and church contributions during the 1960s.

Increasing expenses. The data in table 21 indicate that the operating expenses of our related graduate institutions of theological education increased 147% while church contributions to operating expenses increased only 43%, i.e., *expenses increased 3.3 times more than church contributions.*

Relative decline of church support. Compared to the seminaries,

70

the foundation houses experienced less increase in operating expenses and a higher increase in church contributions. In 1960—61 church contributions underwrote 38.5% of the operating expenses of the seminaries and foundation houses (seminaries 39.3%, foundation houses 30.5%). In 1970—71 church contributions underwrote 22.3% of the total operating expenses of these institutions (seminaries 21.5%, foundation houses 31.9%).

TABLE 21
DISCIPLES THEOLOGICAL INSTITUTIONS:
EXPENSE AND CHURCH CONTRIBUTION TRENDS

Types of Institutions	Operating Expenses 1960—61	1970—71	% of Change	Church Contributions 1960—61	1970—71	% of Change
Five seminaries	$1,153,531	$2,910,478	+152	$453,589	$625,702	+38
Three foundation houses	117,991	233,802	+98	35,999	74,569	+107
Combined institutions	1,271,522	3,144,280	+147	489,588	700,271	+43

This relative decline of church support has forced these institutions to rely more heavily on other sources of operational income, that is, endowment and/or gifts and grants. University-related seminaries have had to rely more heavily on the total income of the university. Those institutions which have a small endowment and receive no financial support from a parent institution have been forced to seek aggressively sizable contributions in gifts and grants from individuals and foundations in order to survive.

Although none of the remaining seven theological schools seems on the verge of closing, the current financial pinch has created a cluster of pressing financial needs for specific institutions.

In general these needs are:

1. Balancing the operating budget
2. Paying an accumulated operating deficit
3. Increasing faculty and administrative salaries in order to support and retain these persons
4. Providing for the addition or replacement of faculty, particularly in the practical fields
5. Providing for creation of new and more expensive programs of instruction, such as supervised field education

Financial solutions. In the present and the immediate future, these pressing financial needs cannot be met without (1) prompt reduction of operating expenses or (2) prompt increase of operating income. The

71

former is very difficult to accomplish given the present circumstances and trends in theological education, as will be indicated later. The latter alternative seems to be the only remaining solution if the Christian Church is to provide a viable professional leadership for the future.

Financial pressures and operating deficits increased through the 1960s and early 1970s. In 1960−61 these pressures and deficits were minimal. As table 22 shows, that year the church underwrote 32.1% of the operating expenses of the seven remaining theological schools. The last two columns on the right of that table indicate what amount was necessary and needed to maintain a 32.1% level of support through the 1960s and early 1970s. They also provide a projected estimate of what funds will be necessary and needed to maintain a 32.1% level of operational support by the church by 1974−75.

TABLE 22

THEOLOGICAL SCHOOLS: OPERATING EXPENSES AND CHURCH CONTRIBUTIONS, 1960−75

Academic Year	Operating Expenses (In Thousands of Dollars)	Church Contributions (In Thousands of Dollars)	% of Operating Expenses	32.1% of Operating Expenses (In Thousands of Dollars)	Additional Contributions Needed (In Thousands of Dollars)
1960−61	$1,231	$395	32.1	$ 395	$000
1961−62	1,421	398	28.0	456	58
1962−63	1,537	441	28.7	493	52
1963−64	1,617	433	26.8	519	86
1964−65	1,624	431	26.5	521	90
1965−66	1,786	466	26.1	573	107
1966−67	2,132	601	28.2	684	83
1967−68	2,332	608	26.1	749	141
1968−69	2,454	641	26.1	788	147
1969−70	2,581	620	24.0	829	209
1970−71	2,942	675	22.9	944	269
1971−72[1]	2,826	689	24.4	907	218
1972−73[1]	3,200	716	22.4	1,027	311
1973−74[1]	3,309	739	22.3	1,062	323
1974−75[1]	3,391	762	22.5	1,089	327

[1] Estimates for these years based on institutional reports made to Commission on Brotherhood Finance in 1972.

In the fiscal year 1970−71, the total church contributed $659,345 to the operating expenses of the seven remaining theological schools. This included all designated and nondesignated monies reported as given by churches to these institutions.

This figure amounts to:

1. 74¢ per participating member for that year, or
2. .5% of the total operating budgets of congregations, or
3. 3.8% of the total church contribution to outreach

If that contribution had been increased by $300,000, it would have amounted to:

1. $1.08 per participating member
2. .8% of the total operating budgets of congregations, or
3. 5.5% of the total church contribution to outreach

If these seven theological schools as a group had received an additional $300,000 contribution that year, they could have:

1. Covered their total operating deficits ($167,702)
2. Increased all faculty and administrative salaries by 10%
3. Provided $25,000 for new programs and methods of instruction

These figures suggest that if the church can approximate a 32% level of support for operating expenses of the seven remaining theological schools and establish a procedure whereby distribution of these additional funds can be directed to points of greatest need, then these institutions can be freed from their most pressing financial pressures and their energies released for developing and educating ministers rather than fighting a growing deficit. Such an increase seems well within the capacities of the church.

E. AMERICAN THEOLOGICAL SCHOOLS

National trends and influences in graduate theological education. The related seminaries and foundation houses, like all other American institutions of graduate theological education, have been influenced by recent trends and forces in seminary education. A brief discussion of some of these may be useful in developing policy suggestions for the future.

1. THEOLOGICAL EDUCATION AS PROFESSIONAL EDUCATION. During the late 1960s and early 1970s, both in the literature on theological education and reforms in the theological schools, there appeared to be a growing common understanding that seminary education ought to be graduate professional education for ministry rather than graduate education in religion or theology. This concept received its most complete articulation in a study by Charles R. Fielding and others published by the American Association of Theological Schools in book form and as a series of articles for *Theological Education*, the journal of AATS. This study continues to influence seminary education.[14]

14. Charles R. Fielding, *Education for Ministry* (Dayton: AATS, 1966).

A more recent and perhaps more prestigious study is the appraisal by Claude Welch of graduate education in religion. Sponsored by the American Council of Learned Societies, the study documents the rapid development of graduate study of religion, largely outside church-related schools and seminaries. *The tone of the report suggests that graduate study in religion ought to be divorced from seminary programs whose principal function is professional education.*[15]

CURRICULAR REFORM. The above trend has produced curriculum reform of field work in many seminaries. Once viewed principally as a means of financial aid, field work has evolved into supervised field education, integral to the educational process and the primary tool by which seminaries seek the curricular balance of theory and practice appropriate to education for the profession of ministry.

NEW FORMS OF THEOLOGICAL EDUCATION. This trend has also produced new forms of theological education. For example, Intermet (Interfaith Associates in Metropolitan Theological Education) in Washington, D.C., funded by the Danforth Foundation, began an experiment in theological education in 1971. A review of current research in theological education and ministry led to the conclusion that "the seminary pattern isolates students from significant learning experiences with groups to whom they must relate as clergymen . . . laity in a congregation, ecumenical peers in the ministry, community leaders and conflict groups, denominational boards and officials, and other professionals like physicians, lawyers, administrators, etc." The experiment is the creation of a program which makes the congregation and community the primary site of education for ministry. The model of education is built around small core groups of candidates for ordination, employed in some form of ministry, supervised by an experienced pastor and lay group who are trained to evaluate the candidate's work. These core groups may negotiate with scholars and teachers in the area to provide needed instruction. An interfaith and interdisciplinary staff is provided to coordinate the program, counsel students, train supervisors, etc.[16]

2. SEMINARY INTERRELATIONSHIPS. A second and related trend among theological schools has been change of the traditional pattern

---

15. Claude Welch, *Graduate Education in Religion: A Critical Appraisal* (Missoula: University of Montana Press, 1971).

16. John C. Fletcher and Tilden H. Edwards, Jr., "Intermet: On the Job Theological Education," *Pastoral Psychology* 22, no. 212 (March, 1971), pp. 21–30.

of small, denominational, independent, and relatively isolated theological schools to consortia, clusters, mergers, and other modes of interrelationship among seminaries. AATS has been an influential force in this trend.

AATS STUDY OF THEOLOGICAL EDUCATION FOR THE 1970S. In 1966 AATS established the Resources and Planning Commission to develop a general plan for the redeployment of resources for theological education in North America. The findings and recommendations of this commission were published in the summer, 1968, edition of *Theological Education.* [17] The study is immensely important for theological schools and should be carefully read by anyone who is concerned with theological education.

OBJECTIVES FOR CHANGE. Following a review of the current needs of the church and the state of theological education, the AATS commission framed a set of objectives for basic changes in programs, methods, and settings:

(1) A new program of instruction in scripture, theology, and history which will aim at developing skills to prepare students to interact creatively and responsibly with the emerging issues of the day, rather than merely learn theological and doctrinal material formulated by others;

(2) A much greater diversity of course offerings and educational methods in this program, so that students with differing educational backgrounds and abilities can find courses of studies adapted to their particular needs and so that they can proceed at speeds commensurate with their varying abilities;

(3) Orientation of the program in a manner to provide professional training in a variety of alternative types of ministries and pastoral situations; training which employs, as a consequence, considerable diversity of new educational methods, instructional personnel, instructional settings, and materials, particularly those which lead to the acquisition of experimental and clinical knowledge; and

(4) The abandonment by seminaries of their traditional attempts of complete institutional self-sufficiency and the direct use by seminaries of

    a. the personnel, programs, and resources of major universities, notably the resources of their graduate professional schools;

    b. the specialized resources (personnel, programs, and settings) available in a wide variety of existing community institutions

17. "Theological Education in the 1970's," *Theological Education* 4, no. 4, supplements 1 and 2 (Summer, 1968). Quotations used by permission of the American Association of Theological Schools.

(governmental, commercial, industrial, and institutional); and
c. certain new training/action agencies (such as the Urban Training Center, MUST, etc.) which combine opportunities for experiential education and practical service.[18]

A curriculum task force of the AATS commission gave an overview of an institutional design that it felt would implement the objectives for change.

The only viable forms of theological education for the foreseeable future will be forms which integrate an intricate array of resources for the purpose of that education. With such an assumption operating, this model needs to be seen first in its broadest perspective, for only then can the contribution of each section of the model be fully understood.

1. The model envisions three levels in theological education. Level I is the level of undergraduate preparation in college or university.
2. The model envisions Level II education as taking place in a major theological center set in a university environment. This theological center would be composed of a number of schools together forming a nucleus, designed to give basic graduate preparation in theological thinking as a foundation for various forms of ministry and Christian involvement in the world.
3. Level III is subdivided into two sections: Level IIIA would provide for vocational preparation in a variety of professional ministries, and would take place in centers related to a nucleus but located where best suited for their particular purposes, usually within the larger metropolitan environment of the nucleus. Level IIIB proposes a new program for preparation for teaching and leadership in theological education. This would take place at a nucleus.

   Together the nucleus and the centers form a cluster carrying on an integrated program of theological education providing a variety of options in professional training.[19]

Model for educational and financial viability. The AATS commission's general conclusion is that if theological schools are to be educationally and financially viable in the future, they will have to be:

1. Located in a major metropolitan area
2. In proximity to a large university
3. Part of an ecumenical cluster of seminaries that *(a)* are linked together in a variety of ways and *(b)* are related to the university in a variety of ways and *(c)* have training programs or centers located

18. Ibid., p. 786.
19. Ibid., pp. 788–89.

throughout the country in the kinds of church situations for which students are being prepared—rural, inner city, suburban, interracial, etc.[20]

Types of clusters. The clustering trend among AATS seminaries has created a variety of organizational patterns that generally resemble one of three types:

1. Corporate merger in which several seminaries unite to form a single new institution that performs all the previous functions of the cooperating seminaries and has a single set of line and staff officers. (For example, merger of Austin Theological Seminary and Union Theological Seminary in New York City.)

2. Consortium of seminaries wherein schools agree upon joint performance of certain functions and/or sharing of certain facilities; but each institution retains its corporate identity and continues most educational programs and functions independently. (For example, Graduate Theological Union at Berkeley, California, or Federated Theological Schools at Chicago.)

3. Creation of a central service agency with which seminaries contract to provide most of the administrative and instructional services traditionally performed autonomously. The participating seminaries retain their corporate identities, boards of control, control over endowments, admission of students, awarding degrees, etc. (For example, the Foundation for Religious Studies at Christian Theological Seminary in Indianapolis, Indiana.)

Fiscal trends. Fiscal trends among AATS theological schools during the 1960s can be summarized as follows:

1. Enrollments remained static or declined.

2. The ratio of students to faculty steadily declined to 12:1 as compared with 28:1 in law schools.

3. AATS seminaries offered some of the most expensive higher education in North America, medical schools being the only type of education more expensive. In 1966 the average cost per student in seminaries was 25% higher than in all other institutions of higher education, 150% higher than in law schools, and 200% higher than in liberal arts departments.[21] Although comparable current figures have not been studied, there is no reason to believe the basic situation has changed.

4. The AATS commission concluded that the high cost-per-student

20. Ibid., pp. 792—93.
21. Ibid. (supplement 2), p. 20.

figure for seminary education was primarily due to the small size of seminaries. Seminaries will still remain small. In 1971−72 the average size of the 187 AATS seminaries was 175 students. Table 23 provides an analysis of enrollment related to size of school.

Seminaries with between 51 and 150 students continued to be most numerous, 43.3% of all seminaries, but having only 23% of the total enrollment. Thus, about 60% of the individual seminaries with fewer than 300 students enrolled 26.2% of all students. In contrast, institutions above 300 enrollment, while comprising only 13.4% of the seminaries, enrolled 41.3% of all students.[22]

TABLE 23
RELATION OF ENROLLMENT TO SIZE OF SEMINARY, 1971−72

Enrollment size	−50	51−150	151−300	301−500	501+
Number of seminaries	32	81	49	16	9
% of total seminaries	17.1	43.3	26.2	8.6	4.8
% of total enrollment	3.2	23.0	32.6	19.8	21.5

5. Seminary salaries remained substantially below those in universities and law schools.

6. Through the 1960s, the number of seminaries experiencing operating deficits increased; yet, generally, seminaries seemed able to increase income at a rate commensurate with rising costs.

7. Traditional sources of support continued to pay the steadily increasing costs of seminary education, with denominations assuming a somewhat larger share than was the case a decade previous.

8. No significant new sources of funding for theological education emerged. Neither foundations nor individual donors became major contributors to seminary education. National church bodies continued to pay only a small portion of the costs of educating persons for ministry in the churches.

9. The pattern of financial support for theological education remained highly decentralized. Main-line Protestant denominations contributed to a pattern of seminary education that remained largely regional and local with respect to finance and control.

10. The consortium-cluster trend among seminaries seemed to slow down some during the latter sixties. Regional identity, institutional

22. *Fact Book on Theological Education 1971−72*, p. 15.

autonomy, and local patterns of support seemed to retard the full realization of the educational and economic values that that strategy holds. In many cases clusters proved to be just as expensive as individual seminaries.

11. On a national scale, the financial problem facing seminaries did *not* seem to be financial survival in the immediate future. The problem was *de facto bankruptcy,* insufficient financial resources to make major educational changes when the current situation facing the church demanded a cadre of well-educated, competent professional ministers.

These fiscal trends of the 1960s have continued into the 1970s, creating financial crises for many American theological schools.

F. GENERAL OBSERVATIONS OF DISCIPLES GRADUATE INSTITUTIONS OF THEOLOGICAL EDUCATION

With the above information as a larger context, perhaps summary observations regarding Disciples seminaries and foundation houses will be useful.

1. PURPOSE: EDUCATION FOR THE PROFESSIONAL MINISTRY. All seminaries and foundation houses indicate that their principal function is education for the various professional ministries of the Church Universal. All have a basic program for the pastoral ministry in addition to programs for selected specialized ministries, such as Christian education, church music, communications, and pastoral counseling.

2. ECUMENICAL CHARACTER. All the programs are interdenominational in character, including the seminaries, which are increasingly interdenominational in the composition of their faculties and student bodies.

3. CLUSTERS AND CONSORTIA. Every institution has some cooperative relationships with other seminaries.
   a. The foundation houses comprise one significant form of clustering. In fact, this organizational pattern appears to offer smaller denominations a method of providing theological education of undisputed excellence that is distributed geographically, in an ecumenical context which enhances and strengthens denominational identity, and economically efficient and beneficial to all parties of the cluster.
   b. Lexington Theological Seminary is one of five seminaries comprising the Theological Education Association of Mid-America

(TEAM-A), incorporated in 1970. The other seminaries are:

Asbury Theological Seminary	Welmore, Kentucky
Louisville Presbyterian Seminary	Louisville, Kentucky
Saint Meinrad School of Theology	Saint Meinrad, Indiana
Southern Baptist Theological Seminary	Louisville, Kentucky

Cooperative programs include mutual library privileges, a joint calendar of guest lectures and concerts, symposia and exchange of faculty, and a January interterm specifically designed for cross-registration of students among the seminaries.

c. Brite Divinity School and Phillips Graduate Seminary are members of the Council of Southwestern Theological Schools, a consortium of ten seminaries in that region. Cooperative programs include mutual library privileges and joint seminars. Since 1972 joint courses utilizing closed-circuit television have been offered in the Fort Worth-Dallas area by Brite, Perkins School of Theology (Methodist), and the Graduate Department of Theology at the University of Dallas (Roman Catholic). Appropriately, the course selected for the pilot project dealt with the ecumenical movement.

d. Christian Theological Seminary led in the establishment of the Foundation for Religious Studies (FRS) in 1969. The purpose of the FRS is to provide a corporate means by which theological schools of varying denominations and churches may, through clustering and other modes of association, pool their facilities, faculties and staffs, libraries, and other resources to enable the highest level of excellence in professional education for ministry and yet retain their integrity and identities as institutions. FRS is a bold attempt to implement the service institution model suggested by the AATS study. *The clustering plan is unique in that it calls for the development of an integrated program on one common campus.* CTS proposes to provide the academic and administrative facilities for the clustering schools on a fee basis, with the other seminaries providing their own student housing. The CTS campus offers an urban setting with geographical propinquity to Butler University, Indiana University-Purdue

University of Indianapolis, and other educational-cultural institutions. At present, FRS includes three seminaries: CTS, the Catholic Seminary of Indianapolis (Roman Catholic), and the School of Theology of Anderson College (Church of God, Anderson). Students admitted to any of these seminaries may take courses from the others.

4. EDUCATIONAL REFORMS. There is considerable curriculum reform and innovation in teaching methods and techniques in all theological schools. Lecture courses are declining; most courses are seminars. Use of travel seminars, field trips, guest professors, audio-visual aids, television, etc., is increasing.

   FIELD EDUCATION. There is a growing recognition of the necessity and value of supervised field education as an integral part of education for ministry. Most students have their field education courses concurrent with other courses. Some, however, take an intern year away from the seminary. Some seminary programs in field education are better developed, coordinated, and integrated with the total education effort than others. Those most fully developed include small action-reflection groups of peers and supervisors (both in seminary and at place of field experience) and opportunities for students to test themselves in several types of ministry. Those less developed assist students in the location of a field assignment but fail to provide programs of supervision in the field by practicing professionals and rely heavily on the student's capacity to create the link between classroom and field assignment.

5. NEED FOR SPIRITUAL DEVELOPMENT. There is a noticeable lack of organized worship, meditation, prayer, and other "spiritual" disciplines on most campuses, although there appears to be some desire on the part of a minority of students to seek such resources through forming small groups. The major problem again is one of integrating spiritual and academic development in the regular process of seminary life.

6. BOARDS OF TRUSTEES. All programs are governed by self-perpetuating boards of trustees. The two university-related seminaries have boards different from those of the parent universities yet legally and functionally related to them.

7. ADMISSION STANDARDS. The admission standards of all seminaries are basically nonselective, admitting practically all students who have a baccalaureate degree from an accredited undergraduate school. The foundation houses, by policies of their

parent institutions, tend to be slightly more selective. A random sample of the undergraduate academic records of 158 students receiving seminary degrees indicates that 90% of the degree recipients achieved average to good grades (C's and B's). A small minority were excellent undergraduate students (10%).

8. FINANCIAL STRESS. All but one of the institutions are currently undergoing financial strain. The relatively large endowment of Disciples Divinity House at Chicago provides virtual economic security. On the basis of operating deficits and cost-per-student analysis, the foundation houses appear to be financially more efficient and manageable than the university-related or independent seminaries. However, the parent institutions with which they are related are experiencing financial pressures similar to those of Disciples-related seminaries, which tends to affect the foundation house programs in a way not always revealed in financial reports.

9. INSTITUTIONAL COMPETITION FOR STUDENTS. There is considerable competition among the accredited seminaries for Disciples students graduating from the church-related colleges and for financial support from churches and church members. The foundation houses and university-related seminaries do not recruit as aggressively for these students as the independent seminaries, relying on their scholarship programs and related undergraduate schools as the primary sources of Disciples students.

10. STRONG REGIONAL IDENTITIES. All eight institutions have strong regional identities and relationships. Each is closely related to the regional church or its geographical area and is an important source of ministerial leadership for small, rural, and other congregations unable to support a full-time, professional minister. Unified Promotion and the Commission on Brotherhood Finance are designed to administer a churchwide, unified outreach dollar. However, the previous financial history of the Disciples influences allocation percentages of that dollar. This results in patterns of church and gift finance for seminaries and foundation houses that are regional and geographical. In addition, student enrollment trends indicate a growing regionalism among the seminary student bodies. These regional attributes often are the primary sources of the institutions' self-understanding and style of education. Thus, even though Lexington Theological Seminary and Christian Theological Seminary are approximately 150 miles apart and Brite Divinity School and Phillips Graduate Seminary are approximately 250 miles apart, each has a regional identity, a regional

constituency, and a regional role in the life of the Christian Church, all of which define the very nature of these institutions.

11. NO RELOCATION PLANS. Perhaps for the above reasons, no accredited seminary or foundation house is currently giving serious consideration to relocating, merging, or closing. As indicated above, Missouri School of Religion has phased out its seminary program as of fall, 1972, in order to use its full resources in the program of undergraduate instruction of religion. Exploratory conversations between Lexington and CTS were held in the mid-1960s regarding possible relocation of one or both seminaries, but no real proposals emerged. Phillips Graduate Seminary has given some consideration to clustering with seminaries in Kansas City, Missouri, or Denver, Colorado, but has decided it has an important mission to fulfill as the only seminary in Oklahoma. It aspires to being an ecumenical seminary giving emphasis to town and country ministries.

12. CENTRAL LOCATION. The seven remaining institutions of theological education related to the Disciples are centrally located in terms of Disciples congregations, membership, and financial support. Table 24 illustrates this point. The data in table 24 show that the seven state regions in which the seminaries and foundation houses are located include nearly one-third of all participating congregations, nearly one-half of all participating members, and nearly one-half of total contributions to outreach programs of the Christian Church. All institutions, except Disciples Seminary Foundation in California, are located within five hundred miles of St. Louis, Missouri. Within a radius of five hundred miles of St. Louis lie all or part of an additional nineteen regions of the Disciples.

TABLE 24
CENTRAL LOCATION OF SEMINARIES AND FOUNDATION HOUSES

	Participating Congregations	% of Total	Participating Members	% of Total	Contributions (in Thousands of Dollars)	% of Total
7 regions of theological schools	1,191	29.4	404,080	44.2	$ 6,762	44.0
Additional 19 regions within 500 miles of St. Louis, Mo.	1,936	47.9	399,728	43.7	6,178	40.2
TOTAL 26 REGIONS	3,127	77.3	803,808	87.9	$12,940	84.2

When these are included with the seven regions above, it is clear that these theological schools are located within the geographical center of the church.

These twenty-six regions include 77.3% of the participating congregations and 87.9% of the total participating membership, and provide 84.2% of the outreach funds from which the Christian Church provides its support of the related theological schools. There is a similar concentration of the twenty-three undergraduate programs in these same geographical areas. Eight are located in the seven-region area; an additional thirteen are located in the twenty-six regions within five hundred miles of St. Louis. Only three, Northwest Christian College, Atlantic Christian College, and Chapman College, are located outside these regions.

The correlation between the presence of these institutions and the relative strength of the Christian Church in these regions suggests that these institutions have made significant contributions to the leadership of the church in their surrounding areas.

G. CERTIFICATION AND ORDINATION

The various regional commissions on the ministry of the Christian Church are the principal agencies in the third stage of ministerial development. Their primary functions are to:

1. Establish procedures to evaluate applicants for ministerial standing
2. Admit persons to candidacy
3. Care for their nurture
4. Authorize ordination and licensing
5. Supervise the act of ordination and licensing
6. Provide vocational guidance and job placement

Most regions have appointed commissions on the ministry, comprised of professional ministers and laity, to coordinate the above six functions. Procedures used to fulfill these functions vary among the regions, but those with active commissions (e.g., Missouri, Northwest, Ohio) tend to have the following pattern:

1. NURTURE. Candidates for the ministry, normally college and/or seminary students, are enlisted by the region, receive communications of interest from the region, and may be invited for an annual visit with the Commission on the Ministry as the major means to nurture interest.

2. LICENSING. If the ministerial candidate so desires, he may receive standing as a licensed student minister, granting him authority for the performance of prescribed ministerial functions within the region. Requirements for licensing usually include *(a)* letters of support from home congregation and institutions of higher education; *(b)* a written personal statement indicating religious background, concepts of the church's purpose and ministry, and career objectives; *(c)* the act of licensing, which takes place in a special congregational service. The candidate is licensed indefinitely, but his status is reviewed annually.

3. ORDINATION. When the candidate nears completion of the graduate seminary program and seeks standing as an ordained minister, the following are usually necessary:

   a. Support letters from home congregation and seminary
   b. Submission of a paper describing in considerable detail the nature of the candidate's commitment to ministry, his concept of church and ministry, his goals in ministry, and description of his education and training
   c. Personal appearance and interview with the Commission on Ministry
   d. Approval by the commission and assistance in the preparation of a service of ordination in the home congregation

Student reaction. Interviews with seminary students indicate that some regions have developed the above procedures more fully than others. Some indicated that they had received no contact from their home region during their entire seminary education. This was more characteristic of students attending seminaries in a nonhome region.

Generally, students expressed more appreciation for the symbol of the church's concern than the value of nurture relationships or evaluation procedures which the commissions on the ministry provided. Interviews also indicated that relationships with the regional commissions were usually initiated by the candidate when seeking candidacy and/or standing. Some who had not contacted their regional commissions had little relationship with them.

H. CAREER SUPPORT SERVICES

The fourth stage of ministerial development includes the variety of programs and services among the three manifestations of the Christian Church which seek to assist the minister in the effective practice of ministry.

Stress in the professional ministry. Mills and Koval recently completed a landmark study on stress in the ministry.[23] Their findings are essential to an understanding of ministry as a stressful profession, the major sources of that stress, and the manner in which most clergy seek to resolve their stress. The implications that Mills and Koval draw from this data are suggestive of needed services among the Christian Church clergy in order to promote greater effectiveness. A summary of these findings and implications follows:

1. STRESS IS COMMON. Career-related stress in the ministry is a common experience—75% of the ministers report it during their careers with frequent "highs" occurring in the years one to five, eight to thirteen, and twenty years after ordination. Implication: Since it is a common and recurrent dimension of clergy careers, *ministers should be prepared specifically to expect and deal with occupational stress, both through educational processes before and after ordination, and through supportive resources available to them.*

2. SOURCES OF STRESS. The largest source of occupational stress for ministers is their job in the local congregation—nearly two-thirds cite it as a cause—growing out of *(a)* personal or ideological conflict with parishioners, *(b)* overwork or lack of achievement, *(c)* conflict within the congregation, *(d)* financial or community troubles of the congregation, *(e)* staff problems, and *(f)* the general feeling that the work of the church is futile or ineffectual. Implication: *Intensive effort in the education of ministers for effective handling of difficult relationships is essential. Because stress tends to arise locally, there should be ample resources provided to deal with it locally.*

3. PERSONAL FINANCES. The second largest source of occupational stress for ministers is personal finances. The need for more money is a serious problem for 26% of the ministers. The major source of stress, however, is relative financial deprivation—the feeling that one's salary is too low in relation to that of members of the congregation, other clergy, or other professionals—rather than the actual salary level. Implication: *Salary problems of ministers are serious, and continuing effort through a variety of means (e.g., multiple-congregation ministries, salary support programs, incentive programs for congregations to increase salaries) is required to ease them.* This is not to remove dedication and sacrifice from ministry, which are intrinsic to

---

23. Edgar W. Mills and John P. Koval, *Stress in the Ministry* (Washington, D.C.: Ministry Studies Board, 1971).

the profession, but to keep voluntary sacrifice from becoming involuntary privation.

4. MARRIAGE AND FAMILY.The third largest source of occupational stress in the ministry is marriage and family based. Marital problems are among the most difficult for a minister to handle. Implication: The intimate relationship between work and family roles in the ministry suggest that *seminary and continuing education should take seriously the training of couples to handle the inevitable marital stresses.*

5. WAYS OF RELIEVING STRESS. To relieve stress, two-thirds of the ministers report self-action (including 24% whose action consisted of moving to another ministerial post) and one-third report seeking out colleagues, superiors, lay people, family, and professional (psychological-medical) help. On the other hand, 40% of the ministers cite colleagues and superiors as most helpful, one-third cite wives. Implication: *Since ministers apparently have a relatively low tendency to seek help from one another, emphasis should be placed upon creating opportunities to build strong supportive relationships among them in which such support can happen naturally.*

6. AGE AND STRESS. Age differences show important variations in the effects of stress among ministers. For example, the futility item is highest among younger men and steadily drops in percentage among older men. The money item, on the other hand, shows most stress among middle-aged men in their forties. Implication: *Age is an organizing variable in the minister's career and suggests differing support services for different age groups.*

7. CONTINUING EDUCATION AND STRESS. The felt need for continuing education among ministers is positively related to the amount of current stress; however, there is no evidence that actual participation reduces stress levels. Implication: *Organization and planning of continuing education curricula to correspond better with points of greatest stress for clergy is needed.*

8. POSITIVE USE OF STRESS. While stress is real and in some cases serious, four-fifths of the ministers reported satisfactory resolution of their difficulties, many indicating renewed strength as a result. Implication: *Stress is both a threat and an opportunity. To turn stress to positive use, the minister must be armed with facts, faith, and a system of well-developed support services.*

Disciples support services. The congregations, regions, and various units and institutions of the general church provide a variety of career support services for professional ministers of the Christian Church. Some of these services include job placement, personal/professional guidance and counseling, health and accident insurance, emergency financial relief, retirement benefits and life insurance, financial advice and tax information, research and studies of ministry, mortgage loans, and continuing education. The principal units providing these services are the employing congregation, the regional church, the Board of Higher Education, the Department of Ministry and Worship, the Board of Church Extension, and the Pension Fund. All these services are important sources of career support. However, because the chief concern here is ministerial education, continuing education will be the service most fully discussed in this report.

National survey of continuing education programs. In 1968 Dr. Connolly Gamble conducted a national survey of continuing education programs for ministry. He identified 766 separate programs of continuing education offered by eight types of agencies:

1. Action training centers
2. Clinical pastoral education
3. Councils of churches
4. Denominational agencies
5. Seminaries
6. Specialized continuing education agencies
7. Universities and colleges
8. Miscellaneous agencies

These programs enrolled 38,401 participants, about 60% clergy and 40% laity. Among Gamble's findings, he noted the rapid development in numbers and variety of continuing education programs from 1960 to 1968.[24]

The United Presbyterian Church and the United Methodist Church have made extensive studies of continuing education for ministry. This report builds on their findings and conclusions in the judgment that the needs, problems, and opportunities confronting ministers of these denominations are similar to those confronting Disciples ministers and generally applicable.

In October, 1968, a United Methodist consultation on continuing education for that denomination's ministry articulated objectives of continuing education for ministry which are commended as appropriate for the Christian Church.

---

24. Mark A. Rouch, ed., *Toward a Strategy in Continuing Education:Proceedings of the Consultation on Continuing Education for Ministers of the United MethodistChurch* (University of Chicago: Center for Continuing Education), pp. 59—72.

The general objective of continuing education is to provide the church with "the leadership of a healthy, competent, effectively performing professional ministry after ordination." To reach that objective, several specific objectives must be met (numbers I-V are change objectives for the individual professional, while VI-X are systems objectives in a continuing education strategy):

I. [Increase] professional knowledge, skills and perspectives necessary to carry out the minister's work.
   A. Development and strengthening of special skills according to his specific calling.
   B. Correcting weaknesses where his specific job requires it.
   C. Knowledge of and ability to use a method of evaluating his effectiveness, including accountability to institutional supervisors.

II. [Promote] perspectives upon the local congregation with which the professional shares ministry.
   A. Theological understanding of the mission of the Church.
   B. Use of the social sciences to illumine the dynamics of congregational life.
   C. Experience in the effective introduction of change and the constructive use of conflict.

III. [Promote] self-examination and personal growth, insofar as these are necessary to professional effectiveness. (This assumes that who and what a minister is affect his professional effectiveness more than in other professions.)
   A. Unifying a self-image in the midst of widely diverse roles and demands.
   B. Inclusion of some continuing education opportunities for the professional's wife.
   C. Inclusion of group and individual therapy resources.

IV. [Provide] data and theoretical perspectives to understand the changing world in which the minister works.
   A. A method of theological reflection.
   B. Knowledge of and experience in using psychological and social processes to minister to persons, structures and issues.

V. [Promote] strengthening of the minister's identity and effectiveness as a man of Christian faith more able to communicate a living tradition to the world.

VI. [Provide] opportunities matching continuing education to the career development pattern of the professional minister.
   A. Specialized training at the proper stage.
   B. Supportive groups and reflection at natural crises points.
   C. Correlation of pre- and post-ordination training.

     D. Major research into career patterns.
- VII. [Promote] the stimulation and support of professional growth by denominational policies and leaders.
  - A. Clear institutional policy encouraging continuing education.
  - B. Use of specialized skills in assignments to boards and committees and charges.
  - C. Appointments on the basis of professional growth needs as well as institutional needs.
  - D. Continuing education for administrative leaders and teachers of ministers.
  - E. Patterns that encourage congregational support of continuing education.
- VIII. [Promote] consideration of professional associations of ministers as a source of support in crises, professional standards and identity formation. (Counseling in career patterns may be done best in this professional context, rather than in the administrative context.)
- IX. [Promote] planning within an ecumenical context.
- X. [Promote] inclusion of laymen in the education and training process.
  - A. Skill training by other professionals.
  - B. Sources of data on professional effectiveness in the congregation.
  - C. Help in reflecting on shared experience in mission.[25]

United Presbyterian study and recommendations. In May, 1969, the Temporary Commission on Continuing Education of the United Presbyterian Church published a 125-page report of its findings and recommendations based on three years of study and research. In summary, it recommended that the church's General Assembly:

1. Approve and adopt a churchwide strategy and program of continuing education for ministry
2. Authorize the development of an organization directly accountable to the General Assembly but primarily responsive to the roles in continuing education of the denomination
3. Approve a plan to work out specific agreements and acceptances of responsibility for different parts of that coordinated program with the numerous organizational structures of the church that need to be involved

25. Ibid., pp. 109–12. Used by permission of the Division of the Ordained Ministry of the Board of Higher Education and Ministry, the United Methodist Church.

4. Authorize a means to facilitate the above actions in cooperation with whatever body is given responsibility for oversight of the reordering of national agencies to serve the denomination[26]

Disciples efforts in continuing education. In contrast to the above, the efforts of the Christian Church for the development of the continuing education of its ministry have been relatively meager. Since 1963 the Department of Ministry and Worship has published an annual catalog of many study opportunities for professional ministers (many of them offered by Disciples-related educational institutions) and annually sponsored a few short-term programs. In the 1967 assembly of the International Convention of the Christian Church a resolution was approved, calling on the church to:

1. Encourage its ministers to participate in the wide variety of continuing education and renewal programs now available
2. Develop specific programs of educational leave for its ministers to include consideration of financial support, length and frequency of such leaves, and a method of carrying on work responsibilities of the person concerned
3. Encourage congregations to undergird the many programs of continuing education and renewal for the ministry offered by colleges, universities, and ecumenical institutions

Subsequently, a promotional piece of material on continuing education was produced for local congregations. In 1969 the Board of Higher Education through its Department of Educational Services assigned one staff member to work part-time in this area and took active membership in the Ecumenical Continuing Education Team (denominational executives of various denominations with responsibilities in continuing education). Since 1969 some modest scholarship support for continuing education has been available through the Department of Ministry and Worship. In spite of this history of effort, however, it is estimated that there has been only a modest increase in the number of professional ministers participating in programs of continuing education.

Needs and resources. In January, 1970, the Department of Educational Services of the Board of Higher Education and the Department of Ministry and Worship made a brief study of the continuing education needs and resources of professional ministers in the denomination.

A representative sample of 343 ministers responded to the questionnaire: 306 were pastoral ministers, 21 were military or institutional

26. *The Report of the Temporary Commission on Continuing Education of the United Presbyterian Church,* May, 1969.

chaplains, 9 were regional-staff ministers, and 7 were other types of ministers.

Some selected results of this study follow:

1. Only 18.5% of the ministers reported that there was a regular policy regarding continuing education leaves in their employing unit.
2. However, 63% indicated that a budget item for continuing education was provided, and 48% reported availability of budget resources for ministerial leadership should they be absent for an educational program.
3. Sixty percent reported that their employers assisted them financially in continuing education experiences during 1967—69. The amount of aid was generally less than $200, but 34 ministers indicated aid of $500 or more.
4. Fifty-two percent of the ministers felt that the ideal continuing education leave was two weeks to a month. But 34% felt that six weeks up to four months was preferable. Forty-three percent reported that one month or less was the maximum time their employers would permit in one program, and 45% indicated that they could have one to three weeks each year for educational leave.
5. Respondents were asked, "What kind of denominational support do you feel would be most helpful to you in your continuing education program at the present time?"
   a. Thirty-one percent gave no answer.
   b. Twenty-four percent indicated more publicity and information from regional and national officers to congregational leadership regarding the need *(not luxury)* of a minister's continuing education. In addition, congregations should be urged to share the cost as a budget item.
   c. Seventeen percent requested scholarship aid for tuition and costs from employing units, seminaries, and the Pension Fund, in addition to regional and national departments of ministry.
   d. Fourteen percent requested more interesting and diversified offerings, including more ecumenical programs.
   e. Some responses indicated a desire that policy guidelines for continuing education be established by appropriate general, regional, and congregational units. Others called for better coordination of available educational programs and specifically for more crisis counseling services, perhaps in career development centers.

Need for continuing education. *In summary, a rapidly changing world, a church in crisis, and a ministry under stress make the need for a systematic and continuing process of education for the professional* *ministry of the Christian Church abundantly evident.* It seems clear that this need demands more than the passage of a resolution, an uncoordinated variety of continuing education programs, and the meager attention of part-time portfolios.

There now exists in the Christian Church the need for:

1. *A churchwide strategy* for the continuing education of all professional ministers
2. *A design for an ongoing program of continuing education,* including provision and recommendation of available programs and resources, in addition to provision of funds and study-leave time to enable professional ministers to participate in these programs
3. The provision of *a full-time office* within one of the general units of the church to promote, organize, and develop the above

This concludes the description of the processes, programs, and institutions of ministerial development in the Christian Church. Although this description has included considerable detail, there is no way that this complex process can be adequately described in a single short volume. If, however, the reader has gained some grasp of the totality of ministerial development in the Christian Church, then the efforts in this chapter have been worthwhile.

5

Evaluation of the Processes, Programs, and Institutions of Ministerial Development

A. READINESS FOR MINISTRY

The complex process of ministerial education that has been described through graduate seminary education moves toward one major goal, readiness for ministry. *This is the criterion by which ministerial education, undergraduate and graduate, is to be evaluated.* The concept of readiness for ministry, as distinct from effectiveness in ministry, is relatively recent in the literature on ministerial education. *Readiness for ministry has been defined by a special AATS task force as that point in the minister's formation when the candidate is adequately prepared for full status as a beginning professional, able to carry adequately the responsibility of ministry while continuing professional growth outside the formal educational setting.* Admission to the office of ordained minister represents the church's evaluation that the ministerial candidate is ready for the practice of professional ministry.

In June, 1972, the American Association of Theological Schools adopted general criteria for the evaluation of the Master of Divinity degree which clearly articulate the components of readiness for ministry.

These are quoted at length with commendation to AATS for its significant work. The Study Commission on Ministerial Education urges consideration of the criteria by all theological schools and regional commissions on the ministry related to the Christian Church.

   A. *Ability to discuss the meaning of the basic documents* (scripture, creeds, systems of order, liturgy) *and heritage* of the religious community in which ministry is intended.

94

B. *Ability to appropriate and explicate a theory of ministry.*
C. *Ability to communicate* through preaching, teaching, writing, or in such other ways as may be appropriate to
1. make creative application of scripture and the religious heritage to the problems of persons and to the crises of society;
2. place contemporary issues in historical perspective;
3. witness to one's faith and commitment; and
4. help people to deepen their relationship to God.
D. *Ability to design forms of ministry* appropriate to particular circumstances.
E. *Ability to function with an appropriate professional style,* which includes
1. interpreting the ministry in the light of theological, historical, and ecumenical dimensions;
2. recognizing one's interdependence with members of other professions;
3. capacity for growth from critique by one's peers in ministry and from other resources in the context of ministry;
4. learning from experience;
5. developing means of transcending personal bias and functioning with a high degree of objective critical judgment; and
6. planning and effecting one's continuing education.
F. *Ability to perceive people and situations accurately and sympathetically.*
G. *Ability to teach,* to train teachers, and to direct the teaching program of the congregation.
H. *Ability to provide leadership* in both the planning and conduct of corporate worship.
I. *Ability to give guidance* where needed, to counsel people experiencing personal crises, or to make appropriate referrals to other sources of professional help.
J. *Ability to function as a change agent*—to use and mediate the range of social process (including conflict) in a way that contributes to the common good.
K *Ability to assist the congregation in the definition and accomplishment of its purposes and effectively to administer its corporate life.*
L. *Ability to discover and use profitably those resources needed in a more effective ministry.*
M. *A spirit of openness to and cooperation with other religious bodies* and traditions, consonant with the mission of church or synagogue.

Program Content and Duration

A. Content (Operational objectives and evaluative criteria)
1. The program shall provide structured opportunity to develop a thorough understanding of one's religious heritage (scripture, theology, tradition) in its current and historical context, and in a way that is functional for one's ministry. Applicable criteria:
   a) Instructional resources are readily accessible to students for developing their understanding of the religious heritage.
   b) Instruction offered is of such quality as will support the purposes and objectives of the institution.

      c) Students are appropriating the religious heritage in such ways as to qualify them for ministry.

      d) Instruction takes seriously the needs of students as persons, the vocation of ministry, and the life and mission of the religious community to be served.

      e) Learning opportunities demonstrate the interdependence of scripture, theology, history, and the social and behavioral sciences.

2. The program shall give opportunity to develop an understanding of persons as individuals, of the social structures in which they live, and of the means of dealing with personal and social crises, within the context of religious beliefs and life. Applicable criteria:

      a) Provision is made for involvement of students and faculty in critical situations within religious and social institutions.

      b) Opportunity is given for disciplined theological reflection on contemporary issues.

      c) Opportunity is provided for persons to develop an appreciation of the resources available in the various sciences and humanistic studies for analysis of and ministry within church or synagogue and society at large.

      d) Provision is made to develop a critical understanding of the various means of dealing with personal and social pathology.

3. Within the degree program or through collateral arrangements there should be provision for experiences in which students may grow in those qualities essential for the practice of ministry; namely, maturity, personal faith, and commitment to the exercise of ministry. Applicable criteria:

      a) Procedures include an adequate counseling program; availability of spiritual counselors; experience in and reflection upon life and service in community.

      b) Instruction is given in the nature and dynamics of spiritual life.

      c) There is careful reflection on the role of the minister as leader, guide, and servant in his community, with particular attention to the spiritual dimensions of the task.

      d) All parts of the educational community are involved in the development of mature personal and spiritual life.

      e) The provisions for personal and spiritual development are integral to the total program.

4. The program shall make provision for exercising various forms of ministry, subject to critical reflection with scholars of the religious heritage, behavioral sciences, and other pertinent areas. Applicable criteria:

      a) Each student secures experience in at least one form of ministry under supervision.

      b) Supervisors are aware of and committed to the school's educational objectives.

    c) Supervising personnel are clearly part of the teaching and evaluative resources with opportunity to assist in the overall design of curriculum.

    d) Professors in the academic disciplines are involved in the process of theological reflection on the ministries performed.

    e) Provision is made for growth in the competence of supervisory personnel.

    f) A significant part of the curriculum is taught in the context of ministry by teams of ministers and representatives of academic disciplines.

    g) Procedures encourage classroom teachers and supervisory personnel to share new understandings on a regular basis.

    h) There are written understandings of responsibilities of students, supervisors, and the institution.

B. Duration

The duration of the course of study will depend upon appropriation of the basic body of knowledge of the religious heritage, development of the professional competencies required as a minister, and formation of spiritual discipline appropriate to the profession. The program will normally require a minimum of three academic years of full-time work.[1]

B. GENERAL EVALUATION

The following evaluation, informed by the work of the AATS task force, is made by the Study Commission on Ministerial Education in the Christian Church and the study director. It includes identification of major needs for adequate ministerial education. Most of the recommendations concluding this volume seek to resolve these needs.

Strengths of graduate educational programs. The seminaries and foundation houses related to the Christian Church are impressive, having many strengths and excellences. Among these are:

1. Competent and dedicated faculties and administrators
2. Openness to curricular innovation and improved teaching methodologies
3. Growing emphasis on field education as integral to the total seminary program
4. Ecumenical dimensions of all schools
5. Cooperative relationships with other seminaries and educational institutions

1. "Procedures, Standards, and Criteria for Membership," *AATS Bulletin* (part 3, 1972), pp. 17–20. (Italics mine.) Used by permission of the American Association of Theological Schools.

6. Dedication to authentic service to the leadership needs of the Christian Church

Weaknesses and needs. There are, however, some evident weaknesses and needs that must be rectified if the professional leadership needs of the Christian Church are to be met and if the current crisis it is undergoing is to be resolved. Some of these weaknesses and needs are:

1. INADEQUATE METHODS OF INTERPRETATION, RECRUITMENT, AND NURTURE. There are inadequate methods by which persons having latent talents, attitudes, and characteristics for effective ministry can be identified, recruited, and nurtured for the profession of ministry. In addition, methods of certification and evaluation for the offices of licensed and ordained minister seem dependent on the interest and strength of individual regions and are, therefore, spotty and uneven. The quality controls in our system of ministerial development seem to be *(a)* the Holy Spirit; *(b)* a limited number of professional ministers, teachers, counselors, and laity who touch the lives of a few persons and guide them into ministry; *(c)* completion of undergraduate and graduate seminary programs of study (which indicates scholastic ability but may or may not indicate readiness for practice of professional ministry); and *(d)* a system of certification for the profession which, at best, entails minimal evaluation of the complex skills, attitudes, and talents comprising readiness for ministry. *We need to develop and implement a churchwide strategy of ministerial formation.*

2. STRUCTURAL AND ORGANIZATIONAL BARRIERS. The current structure of the general manifestation of the Christian Church is a deterrent to the development of a churchwide program of ministerial development. At the present time, a variety of programs for the development and support of ministry are interspersed among the Board of Higher Education, the Department of Ministry and Worship of the Division of Homeland Ministries, the Pension Fund, and the Commission on Brotherhood Finance of the General Office of the Christian Church. The division of labor among these units in the process of ministerial development is not always clear. There is some program overlap between the Department of Ministry and Worship and the Board of Higher Education, which has at times resulted in unnecessary duplication of resources and energies, and has tended to create competing rather than cooperative programs.

PREVIOUS EFFORTS TO COORDINATE PROGRAMS. Twice in the last decade formal proposals have been made to create an administrative mechanism to coordinate the various programs of ministerial formation. One of these efforts led to the establishment of the Advisory Committee on the Ministry, which produced the recently adopted *Policies and Criteria for the Order of Ministry.* Other denominations confronted with similar needs are reshaping their national structures to bring ministry and higher education or ministry and theological education under the same administrative umbrella. *It seems that some general agency or commission is needed to develop a coordinated, churchwide strategy of ministerial education.*

3. EFFECT OF FINANCIAL PRESSURES. Every unit and institution of the church associated with ministerial development is currently undergoing financial stress and pressure. Many of these, with the exception of the Board of Higher Education and its member theological schools, do not place their role in ministerial development as a priority function of their unit. Therefore, without special planning and assistance, congregations, regions, undergraduate institutions, etc., are likely to become less useful in the development of ministry. In addition, increasing financial pressures on theological schools are a powerful deterrent to the continuous reform of graduate education for ministry which the changing needs of the church and society demand. *We need to reorder current financial resources and provide additional financial resources to units and institutions central to the development of an effective professional ministry.*

4. COMPETITION AMONG THEOLOGICAL SCHOOLS. The autonomy and competition among our related seminaries and foundation houses seem to prevent them from cooperating educationally and thereby augmenting and enriching the total system of education for ministry in the Christian Church. This seems to produce unnecessary duplication of program and poor use of total resources, and weakens all institutions rather than strengthening them. *We need to develop cooperative programs of ministerial education among our seminaries and foundation houses.*

5. INADEQUATE COORDINATION OF UNDERGRADUATE AND GRADUATE THEOLOGICAL EDUCATION. There is inadequate coordination between theological schools and undergraduate colleges. Given the growing regionalism of the church and institutions of higher education, *increased communication and coor-*

99

dination among theological schools and colleges having natural ties is needed in order to improve nurture of undergraduate ministerial candidates. For example, graduates and students of Chapman College expressed appreciation for the close coordination with the Disciples Seminary Foundation, stating that it helped them greatly to make a smooth transition from college to seminary.

6. INADEQUATE PROVISION OF EDUCATION FOR ALL TYPES OF MINISTRY. All theological schools have well-developed programs in education for the pastoral ministry. Some have well-developed programs in education for a ministry of music, drama, counseling, communications, Christian education, etc. However, educational programs specifically designed for campus ministry, institutional chaplaincy, social service ministries, bivocational and self-supporting ministries, rural ministry, and ministry among minorities are not provided. *Some strategy whereby students seeking these latter specialized ministries can receive education sufficient for readiness in their chosen ministries is needed.*

This general evaluation and articulation of needs may not be totally comprehensive, but it does identify the major areas of weakness and need in the total process of ministerial development in the Christian Church. It is hoped that this evaluation and the following recommendations are sufficiently comprehensive to stimulate the church to meaningful consideration and response.

6

Recommendations

A. GENERAL RECOMMENDATIONS

In order to summarize some of the observations indicated elsewhere and to articulate the general philosophy of this report, the Study Commission on Ministerial Education presents these general recommendations. These suggestions are addressed to the entire Christian Church rather than to specific units or manifestations of the church.[1] It is our hope these recommendations will elicit a variety of positive responses and actions from various units of the church.

1. **The Development of a Professional Ministry—the First Priority** (see chapter 1)

   We recommend that the Christian Church make its first priority for the next quadrennium, 1974—79, the development of an educated, talented, and culturally diverse professional ministry. Leadership talent of the dimension requisite for effective ministry is available within the rich pluralism of the American society. Persons of diverse cultural, ethnic, racial, and economic backgrounds with leadership talents and qualities must be identified, nurtured, guided, challenged, educated, and supported if professional leadership is to be provided. If the Christian Church is to survive the 1970s with sufficient spiritual and organizational strength to enable it to fulfill its

---

1. To avoid unnecessary repetition, the Christian Church (Disciples of Christ) is referred to as the denomination, the Christian Church, the church, and the Disciples.

ministry to the larger society, it must make the development of high-quality leadership its first priority.

2. **Balanced Education for Ministry** (see chapter 4, B and D)

We recommend that all education for the professional ministries in the Christian Church provide a balance among these dimensions:

a. Scholarly development—acquisition of knowledge and cultivation of an inquiring mind
b. Skill development—acquisition of competence in the practice of ministry
c. Personal development—growth in maturity and the capacity for self-evaluation
d. Spiritual development—growth in personal faith and commitment to ministry

At the undergraduate level, the major task is the acquisition of a liberal education in the cultures of the world and methodologies of learning. There must be provision for experiences encouraging growth in the Christian faith and maintaining contact with the profession of ministry and the institutional church.

At the graduate level, the major task is acquisition of *(a)* a thorough understanding of one's religious heritage; *(b)* an understanding of self, of persons and social structures and how to relate to them; *(c)* growth in one's personal faith and commitment to ministry; and *(d)* the competencies and skills necessary for effective ministry.

3. **Commitment to and Support of Related Undergraduate Programs of Ministerial Education**[2] (see chapter 4, A and B)

Education and nurture of ministerial students at the undergraduate level are essential to the development of an effective professional clergy. Those institutions which have continued viable programs of undergraduate ministerial education, in spite of the church's limited financial support, receive this commission's commendation. The church must continue its support of these institutions, strengthen that support wherever possible, and develop better means of coordinating and encouraging these resources.

2. "Related" refers to educational institutions holding membership in the Board of Higher Education of the Christian Church (Disciples of Christ).

4. **Commitment to and Support of Related Programs of Theological Education** (see chapter 4, C—F)

The Christian Church should continue and strengthen its commitment to and support of its related seminaries and foundation houses. To that end, *we recommend no change in the geographical location of any of these programs at the present time.* Even though these institutions have a long history of operational autonomy, they also have a long history of church relationship and support. Therefore, it would not be presumptuous to recommend relocation if that option, in the church's view, should be confronted.

In the past four years, three related programs of graduate theological education have closed their programs (Drake Divinity School, Disciples House at Yale Divinity School, and the Missouri School of Religion). The locations of the remaining seven are distributed among seven of the strongest regions of the church. Considering the strong regional identities of these institutions, any change in present location might be very disruptive to these institutions and to the regions and congregations they serve. Therefore, the wise strategy at the present time may be to remain where they are, develop ways of strengthening the program of each institution, and develop ways to coordinate the resources of the total group for improved service to the church's leadership needs.

In addition, the AATS report on theological education in the seventies, when proposing clustering as a solution to the financial woes of seminaries, seems to minimize the fact that financial improvement can occur only if *(a)* the financial resources of the institution follow it to its new location and *(b)* duplicative faculty and administration are forced to leave the seminary. The former, given the strong regional patterns of financial support, is very unlikely. Relative to the latter, it should be noted that duplication is often difficult to eliminate.

Because the pattern of merging and relocating seminaries has not, in general, resolved institutional operating deficits, we find little reason to recommend such measures to deal with the financial pressures of Disciples-related theological schools.

Education for ministry among the seven remaining institutions of theological education is basically sound. As a group, they are impressive. All are fully accredited. Growth and change are evident in the reshaping of curricula. All are providing professional education as distinct from graduate study in religion. They are striving to equip

103

and train persons for the complex roles of leadership in the ministries of the Church Universal. In general, the faculty are dedicated, competent, and well-educated men, most having earned doctorates and having some pastoral experience. Primarily due to the introduction of the Doctor of Ministry degree, enrollments have been increasing the past four years. Each institution is involved in a variety of cooperative programs with other institutions of higher and theological education.

5. **Increased Church Financial Support and Influence** (see chapter 4, C)

We are recommending increased financial support of our related institutions of higher education, primarily the seminaries and foundation houses. *Although it may be necessary for the Christian Church to reduce some of its programs and structures, now is not the time for retrenchment of leadership development efforts.* To do so would, in our judgment, eventuate the impotence or demise of the church and the vital ministry it is called to fulfill. Our crisis demands a reorientation of priorities to deal with the root problems of that crisis. Quality education of talented persons for effective ministerial leadership is expensive and will continue to be expensive. It is questionable whether church financial support of graduate theological education at 74¢ per member per year is sufficient for a priority effort.

We are not recommending continuation of the status quo among our undergraduate and graduate programs of ministerial education. Generally, the barriers to the achievement of greater excellence in the preparation of men and women for the ministries of the Christian Church through the related institutions are *(a)* inadequate financial support, *(b)* inefficient coordination of total resources, and *(c)* insufficient influence of the Christian Church on those institutional programs and decisions that involve the church's needs and interests. The total system of ministerial education needs more financial support, a churchwide strategy of ministerial development, and methods providing the church greater influence on the institutional programs of ministerial education.

6. **Ecumenical Education for Ministry** (see chapter 4, C, D, and F)

We recommend that the Christian Church celebrate, support, and implement the ecumenical directions our seminaries and foundation houses have taken. We are in an ecumenical age, searching for adequate expressions of the oneness of the Church Universal. In light of our historic plea for the unity of the Church Universal, it is important for Disciples to do all they can to forward ecumenical theological education. If our seminaries are to survive, if the ecumenical mission of the Church Universal is to advance, we must make adjustments in finance and structure in order to support and implement ecumenical education for ministry.

In addition to the contributions being made to ecumenism by seminaries and foundation houses related to the Christian Church, we affirm also the work of students and faculty working in seminaries not directly related to the denomination. While we appreciate the contributions made to scholarship, ministry, and ecumenism by faculty and students in these interdenominational institutions and institutions related to other denominations, we recognize the need to provide more effective communication, nurture, and support systems more closely relating these persons to the Christian Church.

We, therefore, recommend that the Christian Church explore additional ways to encourage Disciples teaching and studying in seminaries not related to the Board of Higher Education and to integrate these persons more fully into the total ministerial development process of the church.

We also recommend that the Board of Higher Education explore the feasibility of inviting interested ecumenical seminaries to establish formal relationship with the Board of Higher Education.

7. **Improved Coordination of the Process of Ministerial Development** (see chapter 5)

We recommend that the Christian Church accept accountability and clarify responsibility for the total process of ministerial development. Primary responsibility for interpretation, recruitment, nurture, certification, continuing education, and support services for professional ministers rests with appropriate units of the church. Primary responsibility for formal education (undergraduate and graduate) rests with the institutions of higher education related to the church. If the Christian Church is to have a constant supply of qualified, dedicated professional ministers, the whole church and its related institutions must work together. Each unit must do its part in coordination with the others, providing mutual support wherever possible. At the present time, some administrative mechanism must be created to promote that coordination.

B. Specific Recommendations

The following recommendations are directed to various publics, institutions, units, and manifestations of the Christian Church. They attempt to implement the suggestions and directions indicated by the general recommendations.

First Recommendation: Procedure for Consideration of and Response to Specific Recommendations

Directed to: General Board

We recommend that the General Board establish a procedure whereby all specific recommendations will receive official consideration by and official response from all structures of the church to which they are directed.

Second Recommendation: Coordination and Development of a Churchwide Strategy for Ministerial Development

Directed to: A. General Board
            B. Committee on Structure and Function

1. We recommend that a process be initiated which will lodge *coordinating responsibility* for general unit functions of ministerial development in an existing or newly created general unit of the Christian Church. These functions include general unit concerns for enlistment-recruitment, nurture, undergraduate ministerial education, graduate ministerial education, education for women in ministry, education of leadership for the black church and the Hispanic church, education for bivocational ministries, education for specialized ministries, career guidance, placement, and continuing education. We suggest that this unit also be responsible for *planning* a churchwide strategy of ministerial development. This unit should systematically continue the research on ministry begun by the Commission on Ministerial Education, should be responsible for developing methods of evaluation for all units and institutions involved in ministerial development, and should initiate planning procedures that utilize the insights from the varied publics of the church.

2. We recommend that the Structure and Function Committee of the General Board consider uniting these coordinating functions and responsibilities under one administrative unit in the forthcoming Constitution of the Christian Church.

3. We recommend that until the Constitution is developed, an interim

coordinating commission—responsible to the General Board and provisionally lodged with the Board of Higher Education—be established to formulate a churchwide strategy of ministerial development, including selected functions of the Department of Ministry and Worship of the Division of Homeland Ministries, the Board of Higher Education, the Pension Fund, the Council on Christian Unity, and other appropriate units. This commission would develop policy recommendations and suggest procedures such as:

a. How general units, regional churches, and local congregations can cooperate to bring greater unity and clarity of purpose to the processes of ministerial development

b. How to implement the churchwide strategy of ministerial development

c. How to stimulate the creation of innovative programs of ministerial development and education by congregations, regions, general units, and related educational institutions (undergraduate and graduate)

4. We recommend that the coordinating commission include twelve members drawn from the appropriate units, including regions, from the church at large, and with adequate representation of the various publics of the church including undergraduate and graduate institutions, minority groups, women, rural churches, and students preparing for ministry.

5. We recommend that the Board of Higher Education assign a full-time officer to develop and coordinate a churchwide strategy of continuing education for the professional ministry of the church. We further recommend that the interim coordinating commission develop a provisional budget for this office for the quadrennium 1974—75 through 1978—79. We recommend that the General Board request the Commission on Brotherhood Finance to present a feasible method of underwriting this office.

Third Recommendation: Fund for Ministerial Development (FMD)

Directed to: A. Commission on Brotherhood Finance
B. Board of Higher Education
C. Department of Ministry and Worship, Division of Homeland Ministries
D. Unified Promotion
E. Related institutions of higher education

1. We recommend the establishment of the Fund for Ministerial

Development (FMD). The purpose of FMD would be to finance programs of the churchwide strategy of ministerial development proposed by the interim coordinating commission and the unit that succeeds it. The allocation of funds from FMD could be to any program conforming to guidelines and priorities developed by the interim commission and its successor. Such programs can include current fiscal needs of the seven theological schools and other innovative programs of ministerial development and education proposed by congregations, regions, general units, and related educational institutions (undergraduate and graduate).

2. We recommend that the Commission on Brotherhood Finance allocate $300,000 annually to FMD beginning in the 1974—75 fiscal year and continuing through 1978—79, the close of the coming quadrennium.

3. We recommend that the General Board select five persons from the Commission on Brotherhood Finance to allocate FMD monies according to guidelines and priorities established by the interim coordinating commission and its successor.

4. The following suggested sources may be of some use to the Commission on Brotherhood Finance and to Unified Promotion:
   a. Designated contributions from general units, congregations, individuals, and religious foundations
   b. Receipt of growth funds currently distributed to a variety of related institutions of higher education ($35,000 in 1971—72)
   c. Receipt of a portion of funds currently allocated to Bible chairs and schools of religion ($130,376 in 1971—72)
   d. Appeal to all congregations to contribute 1% of their total operating budgets to FMD, above and beyond their outreach contributions

Fourth Recommendation: Development of Endowment for Educational Institutions

Directed to: A. Steering Committee of proposed churchwide finance campaign
B. Christian Church Foundation
C. Related institutions of higher education

1. We recommend that the proposed forthcoming churchwide finance campaign of the Christian Church have as one of its priority concerns the strengthening of permanent endowment funds of our educational

institutions, particularly seminaries and foundation houses, which are most dependent on the church for financial support and are facing severe financial pressures.

2. Recognizing the need of a national strategy for the support of theological education, we recommend the chartering of a "Foundation for the Support of Theological Education of the Christian Church (Disciples of Christ)." Permanent funds should be sought from individual donors and foundations with a minimum goal of 10 million dollars by 1978–79, the end of the coming quadrennium. The income would be used to meet emergent needs of related theological schools and foundation houses not met by allocations from the Commission on Brotherhood Finance. While the funds might be managed by the staff and board of the Christian Church Foundation, the foundation should be separately chartered with the same directors as the Christian Church Foundation as a means of portraying in bold relief the urgency of this cause.

Fifth Recommendation: Alternative Ministerial Education Programs

Directed to: A. Committee on Black Church Work
B. Department of Ministry and Worship, Division of Homeland Ministries
C. Board of Higher Education
D. Related institutions of higher education
E. Board of Church Extension

1. We recommend the establishment of the Disciples Education Extension Program (DEEP). This would be an alternative ministerial education program for persons unable to complete the usual undergraduate and seminary education track. Planning for this program would be developed by representatives of the groups most specifically served in consultation with the interim coordinating commission and its successor proposed in the second recommendation. This program might serve:
   a. lay ministers and laity willing to prepare for bivocational ministries
   b. ordained or licensed ministers without formal professional education
   c. ordained ministers with formal professional education seeking continuing education in their profession
2. We suggest that DEEP be administered provisionally by the Board

of Higher Education in accordance with the strategy of the representative interim coordinating commission.

3. We recommend that primary funding for DEEP be requested from the Commission on Brotherhood Finance. Other sources might include student tuition, FMD, Reconciliation, and grants from interested general units, related institutions, and religious foundations.

4. We recommend that the Northeast Leadership Development Project, currently being developed by the Board of Higher Education, be considered a pilot program of DEEP, receiving the full cooperation and support of all related units and institutions. We gratefully acknowledge the research for this project as the primary source of the concept of DEEP.

Sixth Recommendation: Minority Concerns in Ministerial Education

Directed to: A. Committee on Black Church Work
             B. Department of Ministry and Worship, Division of Homeland Ministries
             C. Board of Higher Education
             D. Related institutions of higher education
             E. Board of Church Extension

We recognize that minority group members in our society are disproportionately exposed to dehumanizing experiences, un-Christian-like treatment by individuals and institutions, and that their continuing alienation from the majority members of society and from the church is inconsistent with the teachings and life of Christ and therefore stand in contradiction to the purpose of the church. We further recognize the fact that having been denied for generations many of the benefits associated with the mainstream of American life, minority groups, as a rule, tend to have different problems and needs, which might require styles of ministry differing in some ways from those required by the white majority. Nevertheless, when we look deeply enough, we see that all men are more alike than different. We discover that Christian Brotherhood transcends racial lines.

1. In keeping with these realities and assumptions, we recommend that theological schools prepare *all* students for effective ministry in integrated situations in a society which sustains, promotes, and exploits cultural diversity.

   a. The curriculum should include courses aimed directly at reducing prejudice, sensitizing students to the unique needs and problems of minority group members, and providing students with skills for breaking down barriers that separate minority and majority group members. (Some possible methods for attaining this objective, in addition to direct course offerings, might be self-actualizing encounter experiences involving racially mixed groups in either on-campus or off-campus situations; exchange student programs with black colleges and universities with relevant course offerings at each institution; and exchange faculty arrangements between black colleges and universities and our seminaries and colleges, securing black visiting professors and lecturers.)

b. In the case of white candidates, a significant portion of the one-year field education (or experience in addition to the one year) should be supervised experience in a predominantly minority congregation and/or minority community.

c. In the case of minority group candidates, a significant portion of the one-year field education (or experience in addition to the one year) should be supervised experience in a predominantly white congregation and/or white community.

d. While doing this portion of their field education, both white candidates and minority group candidates should engage in evangelizing efforts across racial lines.

2. For those students (white or minority) who desire a ministerial career in minority group settings or who wish to focus predominantly upon the uniqueness of the needs and problems of such groups, opportunities for ministerial training commensurate with this purpose should be provided.

a. In consultation with other units, the Board of Higher Education should explore the feasibility of establishing educational programs at predominantly black colleges and seminaries, such as Interdenominational Theological Center at Atlanta University.

b. Again, in the case of black, Hispanic, and other candidates intending to practice ministry in minority settings, we recommend differentiated educational preparation as follows:

(1) For those who are lay ministers, bivocational ministers, ordained or licensed ministers without formal professional education, or ministers with formal professional educations seeking continuing education, we recommend specifically designed programs through DEEP.

(2) For those who prefer to pursue their ministerial education via the traditional undergraduate and seminary programs, we recommend that specific related seminaries be requested

111

to provide educational experiences appropriate to the professional needs of minority students. Of particular importance is the location of the seminary in the vicinity of sufficient minority churches and settings to ensure field education learnings appropriate to the needs of minority churches.

3. In general we recommend that a larger number of black and Hispanic persons be recruited and encouraged to enter all phases of the ministry of the Christian Church (including faculty positions at colleges and seminaries). To ensure their acceptance as legitimate and respected members of the professional ministry, we charge all units of the church—congregational, regional, and general (including institutions of higher education)—to support these persons in terms of education and training, nurture, career guidance and placement. We recognize that this thrust would require substantial financial support.

Seventh Recommendation: Women in the Professional Ministry

Directed to: A. Congregations
B. All units of the church
C. Institutions of higher education

We recommend that a larger number of interested women be actively recruited and encouraged to enter the ministry. In our research it has become very apparent that the number of women active in the professional ministry, seminaries, and related areas is very small and in some cases nonexistent (see chapter 4, C and D). To ensure their acceptance as a part of the professional ministry, we charge that all manifestations of the church—congregational, regional, and general, including the related institutions of higher education—support them in terms of education, nurture, career guidance and placement. Special attention must be given to assignments for field education, placement, and inclusion on seminary faculties.

Eighth Recommendation: Churchwide Policies and Criteria for Ministerial Candidacy

Directed to: Task Force on Ministry

We recommend that the Task Force on Ministry immediately begin the development of churchwide policies and criteria for (1) an orderly admission of applicants to candidacy for ordination and (2) admission to the order of ministry. These policies and criteria would be advisory to regions and congregations. We recommend that these criteria be based on a concept of readiness for ministry in the Christian Church and commend the AATS statement as one document articulating this notion (see chapter 5, A).

Ninth Recommendation: Personnel to Implement Ministerial Education

Directed to: All related educational institutions
(Responses to the recommendation should be directed to the Board of Higher Education.)

1. We recommend that every institution providing ministerial education appoint an appropriate staff person to coordinate all aspects of ministerial development for that institution. This person will provide educational institutions and appropriate structures of the church with a communications link regarding ministerial education. We suggest that this be not less than a half-time assignment and, if possible, full-time. We further suggest that this person have an understanding of and appreciation for the process of ministerial development.

2. We recommend that every institution providing ministerial education form a Ministerial Development Guidance Committee, comprised of representative laity and clergy, to help plan and evaluate the institution's program of ministerial development. We suggest that the committee include representatives of other denominations.

3. We recommend that every institution providing ministerial education give special consideration to the following:
   a. Provision of sufficient exposure to the practice of ministry to maintain realistic appraisal of the function of ministry within the institutional church and within other institutional structures
   b. Provision of opportunities and experiences for the development of religious faith and spiritual life of ministerial students

Tenth Recommendation: Integration of Theory and Practice in Ministerial Development

Directed to: A. Board of Higher Education
B. Regional commissions on the ministry
C. Related graduate theological schools
D. Task Force on Ministry

1. We recommend that all related theological schools give careful attention to the integration of theory and practice in all facets of their educational programs. The upgrading of ministerial education can easily increase the distance between clergy and laity unless theological training is closely related to the actual context of the ministry of the whole church. Different expectations about the nature of professional ministry among seminary professors, professional ministers, and the laity have been documented by our own and other research (see chapter 2, B). In an effort to develop a sense of the wholeness of ministry and better communication between ordained ministers and the laity, we offer the following suggestions:

   a. Every candidate for ordination or licensing should have the equivalent of one year of carefully supervised field education in a form of ministry he or she desires to practice.
   b. Related theological schools should provide trained supervisors, peer groups, and client groups (types of persons with whom the candidate will work in his or her professional practice) as agents of the supervising process.
   c. Students preparing for various forms of ministry should be grouped together so that they are exposed to functional aspects of the total ministry of the church.
   d. There should be wide involvement of practicing professional ministers in the total educational program. Ministers whose effectiveness and professional style are worthy of emulation can be involved in a variety of ways: as guest lecturers, field education supervisors, adjunct faculty, etc.
   e. Related theological schools should provide opportunities for professors to participate in the practice of the pastoral ministry on an extended continuing education or sabbatical basis.

Eleventh Recommendation: Emphases for Curriculum Development

Directed to: A. Board of Higher Education
               B. Regional commissions on the ministry
               C. Related graduate theological schools
               D. Task Force on Ministry

1. In addition to traditional seminary disciplines of Bible study, church history, pastoral care, preaching, theology, etc., we recommend that every Disciples ministerial candidate receive instruction in the theology and methodology of evangelism. Evangelism is a primary

function in both the mission of the church and the practice of ministry; however, this essential task and responsibility has been grossly neglected in the life of the church, in the role and work of the minister, and in ministerial education. It is imperative that special attention be given and major effort made to prepare ministers in the theology and practice of evangelism.

2. We recommend that every Disciples ministerial candidate receive instruction in the history and polity of the denomination. It is most important that candidates understand thoroughly the structures of their church, the process of fiscal support, and other related concerns, so that their ministry will contribute effectively to the well-being of the corporate ministry.

3. We recommend that every Disciples ministerial candidate receive instruction in the history, development, and polity of the ecumenical movement. This is most important, considering the Disciples' ecumenical emphasis and the current increasing ecumenical trends.

4. We recommend that every Disciples ministerial candidate receive at least one unit of clinical-pastoral education or its equivalent.

5. We recommend that all related theological schools emphasize the importance of lifelong learning to effective ministry. To that end, we recommend that every ministerial student be made aware of available resources for continuing education and develop a continuing education plan for the first three to five years of his or her professional ministry.

6. We recommend that all related theological schools seek ways of increasing opportunities for students to continue developing religious faith and spiritual life. We acknowledge that the domain and process of spiritual development is not thoroughly clear, yet its necessity for effective ministry is undisputed.

7. We recommend that each related theological school continue to develop its own style of basic education for the historic functions and enduring modes of ministry. However, there should be cooperative development of special emphases and programs, particularly at the advanced level and/or for specialized ministries or needs of the church—such as *(a)* missions, *(b)* institutional chaplaincy, *(c)* military chaplaincy, *(d)* pastoral counseling, *(e)* nonurban ministry, *(f)* minority ministries, *(g)* religious education, *(h)* higher education, *(i)* church music. We therefore recommend that the Commission on Theological Education of the Board of Higher Education investigate the need and feasibility of developing a master plan of ministerial education which provides the Christian Church with an integrated

cooperative program for specialized ministries. Every effort should be made to avoid unnecessary duplication.

Twelfth Recommendation: Support for Continuing Education

Directed to: A. General Board
B. Division of Homeland Ministries
C. Congregations of the Christian Church
D. Pension Fund

1. We recommend that the General Board request that every employing unit of the church provide sufficient financial support and study leave with pay to allow their professional ministers one continuing education experience each year. We recommend the following minimal program:
   a. A minimum of two weeks per year, with full pay, accumulative to five years
   b. A minimum of $250 per year, accumulative to five years
   c. Financial provision for substitute professional leadership for the duration of the minister's absence

2. We recommend that each congregation, in addition to providing the above financial support, establish a pastoral relations committee whose functions would include:
   a. Encouragement of the minister in setting specific goals for continuing education and professional development
   b. Evaluation with the minister of congregational needs that call for specific kinds of continuing education
   c. Cooperation with the minister in reconciling role expectations when those of the laity and the clergy are in conflict
   d. Regular periodic review of salary, allowances, job description, sick leave, vacations, health insurance, pension, annuity, and provisions for continuing education leave and study funds
   e. Assessment of progress being made in the congregation in the mutual development of a clear concept of ministry in which laity and clergy share responsibility as equals

Thirteenth Recommendation: Study of Ministerial Education Needs in the Northwest

Directed to: A. Board of Higher Education
B. Regional churches in the Northwest

We recommend that the Board of Higher Education, in consultation with the American Association of Theological Schools and concerned regional churches, conduct a study to assess the need and feasibility for additional ministerial education opportunities for Disciples students in the Northwest.

Fourteenth Recommendation: Purpose and Funding of Bible Chairs and Schools of Religion

Directed to: A. Bible chairs and schools of religion

B. General Board

1. We recommend that all related Bible chairs and schools of religion investigate the feasibility of securing financial support from their parent colleges and universities.
2. We recommend that the General Board authorize a study of the current purposes and programs of the related Bible chairs and schools of religion to recommend the appropriate relationship to the Christian Church of these institutions, including financial support.

C. CONCLUDING STATEMENT

These recommendations are offered in a spirit of confidence about the future of the Christian Church and its programs of education for professional ministry. We are convinced that our church will continue its vital witness to the Christian faith and its service to the needs of persons and society.

However, our optimism is tempered by a sober awareness of the challenges that confront us. All the evidence points toward a difficult time ahead for religious institutions in general and ministerial education in particular. Yet, periods of stress can often be occasions for creative response. The work of the Study Commission has been guided by a simple conviction that vigorous, intelligent, and committed ministerial leadership will be of central importance for the vitality of the Christian Church in the future, as it has been in the past. It is our belief that an energetic Christian laity, facilitated by an educated professional ministry, can still constitute a unique avenue through which God will do his redeeming work in the years to come. Such a belief imposes upon our church responsibility inspiring both humility and a special sense of destiny.

With gratitude for the opportunity to address these important matters, the Study Commission respectfully submits this report to the prayerful consideration of the Christian Church.

Appendixes

APPENDIX A

Purpose and Scope of
Study on Ministerial Education
Christian Church (Disciples of Christ)

PURPOSE:
In order to fulfill better God's call for a vigorous professional leadership that will contribute meaningfully to the solution of spiritual and social problems confronting today's world, the Christian Church (Disciples of Christ) and its related educational institutions recognize that changes are needed in the educational processes. This study, therefore, is to:

1. Discover what roles and responsibilities should be entrusted to educational institutions in the preparation of ministers and what roles and responsibilities the church should assume
2. Determine the professional standards by which theological education (undergraduate and professional) is to be appraised; compare these standards with the established criteria for ordination; and recommend desired changes
3. Evaluate the effectiveness of current seminary education for American Disciples ministers, including black and Hispanic ministers
4. Suggest ways that church and educational institutions can be mutually supportive in the preparation and continuing education of ministers
5. Recommend how and where ministers should be educated and trained for the Christian Church (Disciples of Christ)

SCOPE:
The study will encompass a complete and objective appraisal of all aspects of theological education in the Christian Church (Disciples of Christ), including:

1. A thorough description of professional/graduate theological institutions and their educational programs, e.g.:
   a. Institutional histories and development
   b. Number, size, and location of institutions
   c. Accreditation status, admission standards
   d. Organizational and administrative structure

119

    e. Educational goals and objectives
    f. Curriculum and degree structure, methods of instruction, academic calendar
    g. Financial resources, operating budget, sources and control of funds
    h. Student characteristics, attrition, academic quality
    i. Style of campus life and activities

2. An examination of the number and characteristics of undergraduate ministerial candidates in church-related and public colleges and universities. The study will also seek to determine the number of ministers needed by the Christian Church (Disciples of Christ) as well as the various patterns of ministry for which the seminaries are preparing persons.
3. A survey of continuing education of ministers, available programs, enrollment of Christian Church (Disciples of Christ) ministers, and the general value and effectiveness of these programs.

May, 1971
(Revision)

APPENDIX B

Sources of Funding

Board of Higher Education	$ 6,500
Canfield Trust	1,500
Christian Board of Publication	5,000
Individual	100
Oreon E. Scott Foundation	5,000
Seminaries/Foundation Houses, Christian Church	6,400
Unified Promotion	15,500
	$40,000

APPENDIX C

Study Commission Roster

1. COMMISSION MEMBERS

Chairman:
Dr. Frank G. Dickey
Executive Director
National Commission on Accrediting
Washington, D.C.

Study Director:
Mr. Carroll C. Cotten
Candidate for Ph.D.
  in Higher Education
Stanford University
Palo Alto, California

Vice-Chairman:
Dr. Donald S. Browning
Associate Professor of
  Religion and Personality
Divinity School, University
  of Chicago
Chicago, Illinois

Ex officio:
Dr. William L. Miller, Jr.
President
Board of Higher Education
St. Louis, Missouri

Rev. C. William Bryan
Minister, Central Christian Church
Indianapolis, Indiana

Mrs. Eleanor Mayhew
Laywoman
Cleveland, Ohio

Rev. M. Glynn Burke
Minister, Central Christian Church
Lexington, Kentucky

Dr. Lawrence E. Pitman
Executive Secretary
Northwest Regional Christian
  Church
Seattle, Washington

Dr. Alex J. Cade
Professor of Counseling and
  Educational Psychology
Michigan State University
E. Lansing, Michigan

Rev. Charles Watkins
Minister, First Christian Church
Carbondale, Illinois

Dr. D. Ray Lindley
Chancellor
University of Americas
Puebla, Mexico

Dr. Matthew E. Welsh
Attorney at Law
Indianapolis, Indiana

122

2. SUPPORT STAFF

Rev. Ralph E. Glenn
Vice-President for Program
  and Development
Board of Higher Education
St. Louis, Missouri

3. CONSULTANTS

Dr. John R. Compton
Minister, United Christian Church
Cincinnati, Ohio

Dr. Edgar W. Mills
Director
Ministry Studies Board
New York, New York

Rev. Dr. Paul A. Crow, Jr.
General Secretary
Consultation on Church Union
Princeton, New Jersey

Rev. Lester D. Palmer
Vice-President-Secretary
Pension Fund of the Christian Church
Indianapolis, Indiana

Rev. Thomas E. Wood
Executive Secretary
Department of Ministry and Worship
Indianapolis, Indiana

APPENDIX D

Central Issues and Questions for the Study of Ministerial Education

1. Nature and structure of the Christian Church (Disciples of Christ) and its ministry
   a. What are the major characteristics of the professional ministry of the Christian Church?
   b. What are the characteristics of effective ministry in the Christian Church today? Can they be identified and, if so, how measured? Are these characteristics reflected in the standards, criteria, and procedures for ordination of Disciples ministers?
   c. In light of sociological and ecclesiastical trends, what will the shape of the Christian Church and its ministry most likely be in 1980–90?
   d. What are the major current and future needs for an effective professional ministry? Are there and will there be enough ministerial candidates? Are they of sufficient quality to meet the standards for an effective ministry? What professional skills need to be strengthened most?
2. Institutional roles and responsibilities in the preparation of ministers
   a. What roles and responsibilities are currently assumed by the church and its related educational institutions in the preparation of ministers?
   b. In light of current trends in higher education, what changes and shifts are likely in these roles and responsibilities?
   c. What roles and responsibilities should be assumed?
3. Appraisal of current theological education
   a. What are the stated goals and purposes of Disciples seminaries? Is there general agreement among various. constituents of the Christian Church regarding the purposes of Disciples seminaries? If not, what are the nature and locus of the disagreement and how can the desired direction of ministerial education be established? In light of the nature of seminary education and the current and future needs for professional ministry, what should the educational goals of Disciples seminaries be?
   b. Are Disciples seminaries educationally and financially sound? Can the Christian Church continue the current level of financial support of seminaries? If not, what are the future implications for change?
   c. What are the principal strengths and weaknesses of the ministerial education program in Disciples seminaries? Are the seminaries providing an educational program sufficient for Hispanic and black ministers? Women?

    d. What interinstitutional arrangements among seminaries, colleges, and universities currently exist? What do these contribute to ministerial education?

    e. In general, is the current undergraduate education of ministerial candidates adequate preparation for seminary education?

    f. What types and numbers of ministers are involved in what forms of continuing education? How useful do they feel this education is for their ministry? What roles, responsibilities, and support should the church and seminary assume in the provision of continuing education?

4. Policy recommendations

    a. To enable the study to make significant impact on the policy and programs of ministerial education in our denomination, what political and structural realities and sensitivities must be recognized and considered?

    b. What changes should be made in the educational programs of our seminaries to improve ministerial education?

    c. What restructuring of financial support, relocation of educational institutions, and interinstitutional relationships with colleges and universities would enable a more efficient and effective educational program in Disciples seminaries?

    d. How could the church and educational institutions be mutually supportive in the preparation and continuing education of ministers?